THE SONG OF A MERRYMAN

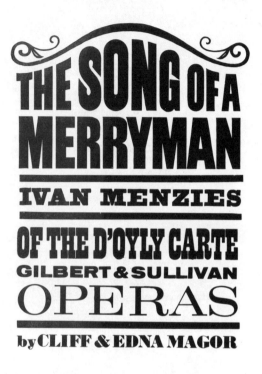

THE SONG OF A MERRYMAN

IVAN MENZIES

OF THE D'OYLY CARTE
GILBERT & SULLIVAN
OPERAS

by CLIFF & EDNA MAGOR

GROSVENOR BOOKS

FIRST PUBLISHED 1976
BY GROSVENOR BOOKS
54 LYFORD ROAD
LONDON SW18 3JJ

© *Cliff and Edna Magor 1976*

*Front cover: Ivan Menzies
as Jack Point in
'The Yeoman of the Guard'*

*Back cover: Ivan and Elsie Menzies
as Robin Oakapple and
Rose Maybud
in 'Ruddigore'*

Cover design by Cameron Johnson

ISBN 0 901269 18 2

PRINTED IN GREAT BRITAIN BY TONBRIDGE PRINTERS
TONBRIDGE KENT

Contents

Preface

An Australian lover of the Gilbert and Sullivan operas, waiting for the curtain to rise on a centenary performance of *Trial by Jury* at the London Savoy on 9 April 1975, turned to his neighbour, a complete stranger, and remarked, 'I wonder what became of Ivan Menzies? He *was* Gilbert and Sullivan to us'.

Minutes later he was delighted to see the stocky figure of his favourite comedian on the stage. With Ivan was his wife, Elsie Griffin, the leading soprano of those far-off days and as famous as Ivan himself in many countries. They had been asked to sit with the jury for this unique performance and when introduced to the audience were greeted with a torrent of applause.

It was over fifty years since they had first appeared together in the D'Oyly Carte Companies. Elsie, a child prodigy, who later sang for the forces in World War I such songs as *Roses of Picardy* which was written specially for her, was already a great star when Ivan joined the Company as a trainee. She often could not leave the theatre for the crush of fans and her HMV record of *Poor Wandering One* was judged the best British-made disc of 1930. By the late thirties Ivan had established himself as the most popular Gilbert and Sullivan star in Australian and New Zealand history.

Ivan and Elsie had married in secret and repented openly, often quarrelling fiercely on stage up to the moment when the curtain rose to show them as two sweetly smiling lovers. They had just got to the point of divorce proceedings when, amazingly, they began to find their long way back to happiness.

A change had come about in Ivan's character which surprised his fellow actors and riveted the attention of the Australasian public. The ten years during which he toured Australia and New Zealand were a formative period for those nations. They had struggled out of the Depression of the thirties into the war of the forties. What Ivan brought strengthened the national leaders and helped to sustain the spirit of the people.

We knew Ivan well, for Edna was his secretary at one time. It was his gaiety and directness which captured so many of us. He carried his new-found Christian faith off stage and on with the same elan which kept the theatre audience rolling with laughter at his Ko-Ko or near to tears as he played Jack Point. It was fun to be with him then, and it is still so today. After more than fifty years together, he and Elsie, although no longer in the limelight, retain the same infectious qualities which captivated the public so many years ago.

We should like to acknowledge the help given to us by many friends who knew Ivan Menzies, and in particular to thank Vera Frampton and Garth Lean for their editorial advice.

CLIFF and EDNA MAGOR

South Australia, 1976

1

Faint heart never won fair lady
—Iolanthe

Ivan Menzies made his first professional appearance in the chorus of the D'Oyly Carte Company at a charity matinee of *HMS Pinafore* in Manchester in March, 1921. He was then twenty-five years of age. Just before the show he caught sight of the leading lady, Elsie Griffin, standing outside the theatre selling pictures of herself for the charity. In her mauve frock and black picture hat she seemed to him even lovelier than when on the stage. He fell in love. The only way he could think of to attract her attention was to empty his pockets of all he had in exchange for a photograph. She was impressed, and began to talk to him. He was quite determined to marry her although at the time nothing seemed less likely.

Ivan was the son of a Lake District doctor. He had been a high-spirited boy, spoilt by indulgent parents, and involved in all sorts of escapades. His school record was poor, with more interest in truancy than in study. He had bumbled through various jobs—playing the piano in his cousin's cinema was the longest-lasting—until the war took him to the Western front. On 8 August 1916 in the Battle of the Somme his right arm and thigh were shattered and he was invalided out. Work was hard to find. The best job he could get was with a market gardener at £1 a week. He lived in a caravan big enough to take a six-octave piano at which he played and sang for hours, hoping to catch the attention of some famous impressario, but nothing happened.

From a very early age he loved amateur theatricals, and it was after playing Sir Joseph Porter in a village musical society's *HMS Pinafore* that he decided to try his luck at an audition with Mr Rupert D'Oyly Carte at the Manchester Opera House. His appearance at this charity matinee was his first trial.

Elsie Griffin had been in the Company for two years and was a star of dazzling brilliance. She had first made her mark singing to the troops in the latter days of the war, and two famous songs, *Danny Boy* and *Roses of Picardy*, had been written for her. After her first London performance as Mabel in *The Pirates of Penzance*, the crowds at the stage door were so dense that she had to be escorted through by the police. It was the same night after night, and in those early years she always ate sandwiches between matinees and evening performances rather than attempt to leave the theatre. King George and Queen Mary came regularly to hear her.

Such was the girl on whom Ivan set his eye. But he was never lacking in self-assurance. Certain that one day he would play the principal parts, he watched the incomparable Henry Lytton closely and secretly learned his roles. A year later, D'Oyly Carte formed a second company and made Ivan understudy to the principal comedian, who obligingly fell ill almost immediately. Appearing at a moment's notice, he delighted the audience by his agility and wit, and by his original little dances. The manager telegraphed to D'Oyly Carte to come up from London to see him.

Ivan was on his way to fame, but he was separated from Elsie—and he had many rivals. He agitated to return to the Repertory Company in which she played, and when he got there, started making his feelings clear. He proposed to her in the wings, in the dressing room, in the cinema, and in a picturesque ravine where he threatened to throw himself over the cliff if she refused him. She was amused by such heroics but continued to turn a deaf ear. Then one day, as they walked together in Sheffield, Ivan went ostentatiously up to a policeman, and after talking to him for a moment returned to Elsie without a word of explanation.

'What were you saying to that policeman?' she asked when she could restrain her curiosity no longer.

'Oh', he replied casually, 'I just asked him the way to the Registry Office. I thought we might drop in and ask about a special licence.'

'We will do nothing of the sort', Elsie replied hotly—but they did, and were married three weeks later on 9 March 1923. They had decided to keep their wedding secret because news of it would have attracted unmanageable crowds of curious spectators. They thought too that D'Oyly Carte was likely to disapprove. They were playing in Leeds at the time, but travelled back to Sheffield for the wedding.

At the railway station they had their first tiff. The members of the Company made it a custom to share expenses equally on outings, and Ivan maintained that Elsie should pay her own fare to Sheffield, while he would pay for both on the return journey as man and wife. Elsie expected something more gallant from her bridegroom on their wedding day and objected strongly.

Ivan was adamant and Elsie yielded with a bad grace. Not even the mauve frock and black picture hat which she was wearing at Ivan's insistence could make her look the radiant bride as the train carried them to Sheffield.

The only guests were Elsie's best friend and her parents, both of whom had opposed this wedding. Ivan knew that they did not approve of him. Perhaps they had never forgotten the day when he nearly fell through the roof while persisting, against their wishes, in trying to put up a wireless aerial! He still had to make his way in the world, and they did not consider him worthy of their famous daughter. They were waiting at the Sheffield railway station and looked to Ivan as though they had met for a funeral rather than a wedding. The Registrar performed the ceremony and Ivan gave him a little silver spoon which the jeweller had thrown in with the wedding ring. As the party left the office Elsie's mother turned pale at the sight of the ill-omened street name on the wall opposite—Workhouse Lane. Ivan brushed this lightly aside with the far from reassuring remark that he had often been down to his last penny but something had always turned up. Rain began to fall and the gloom deepened.

The couple returned to Leeds but continued to live in separate digs in order to keep their marriage secret. The truth soon leaked out, however, and Ivan thought it wise to tell D'Oyly Carte. He was now understudying Henry Lytton and doing comedy roles. He was even given an occasional performance in Lytton's parts, although this meant that Sir Henry, who had never been off for years, had to be asked to stand down.

A happy period followed. For their first holiday together Ivan bought a speedboat, and disturbed the quiet hills of the Lake District with its roar. He had acquired this boat from one of his rivals for Elsie's hand, the son of a mill-owner who disapproved of his son's interest in an actress. The mill-owner had been so relieved when Elsie married Ivan that he had bought his son a Rolls Royce and a speedboat. The boat did not appeal to the young man, who offered to sell it to Ivan.

'No', said Ivan, 'I can't afford it.'

'Well, make me an offer', the other replied.

More as a joke than anything else Ivan offered five pounds. 'Right, it's yours', and Ivan was the proud owner of a speedboat.

For some time all went well, but Ivan grew dissatisfied with being an understudy. He was now well-established and in a position to drop hints that unless he was offered something more satisfying he might have to try fresh fields. At the end of the tour he was offered the position of principal comedian in the New D'Oyly Carte Company.

He had now reached the place where he had dreamt complete satisfaction was to be found, with himself as leading man and Elsie as leading lady. But perfect happiness still eluded him. One of the causes was artistic temperament, which Ivan now describes as 99% temper and 1% artistry, but which at that time he considered one of the characteristics of genius. Sometimes the happy couple took several days to get over an argument. They argued in bed at night till three or four in the morning over some point, each unwilling to go to sleep for fear the other might get the last word.

It is easy to see some of the causes of their incompatibility. Ivan was the eldest son, who received much affection but very little discipline. He expected Elsie to wait on him hand and foot as his mother had done. He also expected her to be demonstrative in her affection for him. Elsie was the only child of hard-working undemonstrative parents and could not show affection easily. Her family had had a struggle economically. She had started work at fourteen, and knew the value of every penny, whereas Ivan's life had been made easy by his father's generosity, and he had not learnt to handle money carefully. Both had strong wills and both were stars accustomed to the spotlight in the centre of the stage. It is not surprising that they clashed.

In 1926 a daughter was born and named Mahala. In the same year the New D'Oyly Carte Company was disbanded. Ivan now found himself in a small London flat with a wife and child and no regular work. For a time he was an 'Uncle' in a BBC children's programme.

Elsie was unhappy because she found managers suspicious of leading ladies who had babies, thinking it would lessen their box office appeal. Ivan's remark that a woman's voice lost its freshness after thirty was not helpful, to say the least.

He thought her nerves must be in a poor state—why otherwise should she be annoyed when he went on hammering nails into a wall after she had asked him to stop? Once he had dreamed of playing her accompaniments. But now, as they practised for radio broadcasts and London concerts, the voice that had once enraptured him got on his nerves. Rehearsals often ended in quarrels. At times they were quarrelling

Elsie Griffin, leading soprano of
the D'Oyly Carte Company,
as Phyllis in *Iolanthe*

Ivan Menzies admired Elsie
—at first from afar

Ivan in his speedboat
on Lake Windermere
where he and Elsie
spent their first
holiday together

**Evelyn Gardiner as Katisha
and Ivan Menzies as Ko-Ko
in *The Mikado***

photo: Howard Short

**Ivan Menzies' interpretation
of Ko-Ko underwent many
changes, which theatre critics
were quick to notice**

fiercely up to the moment the curtain rose and showed them sweetly smiling for the benefit of the audience.

Not much money was coming in and Ivan had difficulty in paying the rent. He had spent nearly all his savings on furnishings and a new car, for which he had also borrowed from Elsie. The situation improved when he got principal parts in *No, No, Nanette, Happy Go Lucky* and *Charley's Aunt*. He toured for several months while Elsie stayed at home and looked after Mahala.

Ivan was no happier, but Elsie found her irritation growing into a strong resentment against the callous, self-centred man who was her husband. After all, it was Elsie Griffin that the King and Queen used to come to hear. She was not much distressed or surprised when Ivan accepted an offer to tour Australia and New Zealand as principal comedian in a Gilbert and Sullivan Opera Company formed by J C Williamson, Ltd, showing no compunction about leaving his wife and daughter. Elsie sold the home, stored the furniture, and arranged for her mother to look after Mahala while she went back to the stage.

2

Yet everybody says I'm such a disagreeable man,
And I can't think why

—Princess Ida

For Ivan the invitation to Australia was an unexpected chance to begin life afresh. Professionally he was completely self-confident. He had thoroughly mastered the comedian's art; had learnt to use an uncertain voice to good advantage, and was at thirty-four as light on his capering feet as he had ever been. He was good at his job and he knew it. He determined to take the people 'down under' by storm.

At the press conference on arrival he appeared properly modest about earlier successes. Asked what he thought of Australia he replied, 'It's not what I think of Australia that is important, but what Australia thinks of me.'

When the Company opened in Melbourne there was no doubt about their success. The well-worn but ever-fresh lines of Gilbert, with their gentle humour at the foibles of unchanging human nature, gave Australian audiences a chance to laugh kindly at Britain, the mother country which they still respected. Laughing, they took Ivan to their hearts. His triumph was immediate. He was intensely happy. He took a flat, where he gave bright parties which always included many pretty girls, who found him as amusing off the stage as on it. His frequent hang-overs were worked off on the golf course, where he made many friends.

The Company moved on to Sydney. Here he loved the sun and surf at Manly and Bondi, and found a millionaire only too happy to take him on the harbour in his yacht. There were always plenty of adoring girls to make a fuss of him and play bridge till the early hours of the morning while he 'ran down' after the show. For exercise there were always tennis courts available.

Not everyone enjoyed life as much as he. The Stage Manager, Richard Shortland, who had to bear the brunt of his temperamental outbursts, once said that he expected to go to heaven because he had had his hell on earth. In his thirty years' experience he had never had to handle a more disagreeable artist. Everybody was expected to give way to him; he had scant consideration for fellow-artists, but if anyone offended against the great Mr Menzies there was a stormy protest to the Stage Manager. If, however, Mr Menzies was spoken to about his breach of stage etiquette he would reply in his most lordly tone, 'If you don't like it put the understudy on', knowing his own popularity with the public made it impossible to do so without a serious effect on the box office.

The principal contralto, Evelyn Gardiner, who played opposite Ivan Menzies and recognized that he taught her a good deal of stagecraft, says that he cared for no one but himself. Only the best was good enough for him, and no matter who or what stood in his way, he intended to get it. He was quarrelsome and mean in the small details of everyday life. One is reminded of King Gama in *Princess Ida* who couldn't think why he was regarded as such a disagreeable man. When Ivan

Menzies sang that song there were plenty in the Company who could have enlightened him.

The public, however, found him highly agreeable. Press reports both in Australia and New Zealand could scarcely have been more favourable. In the Adelaide *Advertiser* Dr Alex Burnard, a critic who was often considered unduly harsh, wrote, 'I do not think that people who laugh, and permit themselves to laugh, ever have laughed with quite such abandon as they did at Ivan Menzies as the Lord High Admiral in *Pinafore*. I myself was incapable of making any notes for some time.' After seeing *Iolanthe*, he added, 'Ivan Menzies, as he always does, did what he liked with us.'

Reading through a collection of press notices, one comes to expect such phrases as 'dapper performance', 'agility and dexterity', 'a completely individual style'. Many times the writer had been 'surprised'—surprised at the tragic intensity with which he played Jack Point, surprised at the excellent quality of his singing of 'Tit Willow', surprised at his restraint in the part of Schubert in *Lilac Time*. 'Mr Menzies is a comedian from whom surprises are always to be expected', the Melbourne *Argus* stated in its review of *Trial by Jury*, 'but nobody expected him to produce a yo-yo.'

Although Ivan Menzies could have the house in fits of laughter merely by appearing on the stage and holding up a little finger, and was sometimes criticized for over-exuberant buffoonery, his favourite role was the more serious Jack Point in *The Yeomen of the Guard*. 'Features, gestures, actions and words were perfect in Mr Menzies' masterly interpretation of the role', the *Otago Daily Times* reported. 'With infinite skill and

finesse he prepared his audience for what was to come...
He proved himself an artist of real and extensive merit.'
In the opinion of the *Dunedin Star* Mr Menzies 'ranked
with the greatest Jack Points they had seen'. 'He gave
us', it said, 'a delineation of sheer artistry in every detail'.

One feature which often drew comment was the
clarity of his enunciation. As early as 1928 the London
Evening News remarked that Henry Lytton had said he
had never heard better rapid enunciation than when
Mr Menzies sang the Lord Chancellor's 'patter' song.
The same 'perfect enunciation both in singing and
speaking' was noted by an Australian paper a few years
later.

Conservative critics would sometimes criticize Ivan
Menzies for taking liberties with the scripts and making
some allusions more topical when the traditional ones
had no meaning for Australians. He defended himself
against such criticism by pointing out that there are
several instances in the operas where Gilbert left in-
structions that names and places should be localized.

The part most often criticized was his Ko-Ko in *The
Mikado,* for being too boisterous, but he maintained that
Gilbert had specially called him a buffoon. 'So', he said,
'I play Ko-Ko as a buffoon.' 'It was never meant', he
claimed, 'that any character in these operas should be
stereotyped. The operas would never have survived if
they had.'

Following seasons in Melbourne and Sydney the
Company had crossed to New Zealand, and the critic
in the country town of Invercargill wrote what must
have been one of the most devastating criticisms Ivan

Menzies had ever received. He began by making critical remarks about his performance in *The Gondoliers*.

'I'll show him', Ivan muttered to himself. 'I'll give him something to write about tomorrow night when we play *The Mikado*.'

The next night he really extended himself and kept the audience rolling in mirth. He did everything except fall through the drum. Next morning he opened the paper expecting to be attacked in at least half a column, only to find that the critic had written a good column in praise of the other members of the cast, one by one, and then added as an after-thought, 'Ivan Menzies played Ko-ko, when he was not getting in the way of those playing *The Mikado*.' The next time he performed *The Mikado* Ivan played absolutely to tradition, even to retaining the traditional references, and got so few laughs that the directors came to him and said, 'For God's sake play it as you always do.'

Occasionally departure from tradition was accidental. One night Evelyn Gardiner, who was playing Katisha in *The Mikado*, and whose commanding figure towered above Ko-Ko, swept her arm round with a majestic action just at the right height to strike his top-knot accidentally and knock his wig off.

'Ah', said Ivan, 'so you'd scalp me, would you?' and in a loud aside to the delighted audience he added soothingly, 'Keep your hair on.' This further convulsed the audience.

The same quick wit came to his rescue on the night he was grovelling on the floor trying to appease Katisha, and put his hand on a number of carpet tacks that had been left scattered there. Holding up his hand with several of them clinging to it, he remarked, 'Tax on everything'.

Another accident, which was more serious for the actor involved, occurred during *H MS Pinafore*. The restraints of tradition are cast aside during encores, and one night as one after another of 'Never mind the Why and Wherefore' was demanded, Ivan's antics became more and more hilarious. He directed the ancient canon on the deck at the audience and finally, probably from sheer exhaustion, sat on the rope that surrounded the companion-way. Gregory Stroud (Captain Corcoran), having finally caught up with his Admiral, sat down with him. Under the weight of the two men, the rope gave way, and Stroud fell through the hatch with a heavy thud. He must have been the only one in the theatre who was not amused, and if the Captain thought this was one of those rare occasions for a 'big, big D', the uproar drowned it.

From New Zealand the Company returned to Brisbane. Here he loved the warm sunshine in the middle of winter, and found the audiences as warm as the climate. It was the early 1930s, the time of the Great Depression, and many people wrote to tell him he was a ray of sunshine in the gloomy days.

There was no doubt that he had done a good job. When the Gilbert and Sullivan Company left Melbourne after the first season to move on to Sydney, one paper was certain that it could have continued for many more weeks. 'Never in Australian stage history', it said, 'has there been such a successful Gilbert and Sullivan season as this.' 'And never', the Stage Manager might have muttered, 'have I had a more difficult one.'

3

Stern conviction's o'er me stealing
—HMS Pinafore

As the Company travelled along the lovely Pacific coastline of North Queenland to Cairns, Ivan had seen a picturesque tropical island, Bedarra, four miles off the coast from the mouth of the Tully River inside the Barrier Reef. He visited it and found it a near paradise, about three miles in circumference, with an oyster bed, coral gardens, silver beaches and waving palms. Immediately he wanted to own it. In his mind he planned a little kingdom where he could reign supreme, and give the parties for which he was becoming famous.

It took him six months to track down the owner who was living in Nice. He did not want to sell it, as he intended to leave it to Dr Barnardo's Homes. Ivan told him that he was planning to bring out some poor boys from the East End of London and give them a fresh start, and so got him to agree to let him have it for £500. Ivan was excited when he got the title deeds: visions of girls with ukeleles mingled with schemes for 'good works'.

Meanwhile he had met a woman in Australia who really seemed to understand him. In his letters home to Elsie in England he began to try out her feelings on divorce. He told her that if she still cared for him at all, he would stand by the marriage contract. Her answer was that his letters about the other woman had already been passed to her solicitors.

To salve his conscience, perhaps, he got Elsie an engagement as prima donna in a South African tour of Gilbert and Sullivan, in which he was playing on his way home to England. Once more she took her place opposite him in the familiar roles. They met night after night as Yum-Yum and Ko-Ko, or as Rose Maybud and Robin Oakapple, the simple farmer turned bad baronet in *Ruddigore*. One night they spoke the familiar words:

'Rose, when you believed that I was a simple farmer, I believe you loved me?'
'Madly, passionately!'
'But when I became a bad baronet, you very properly loved Richard instead?'
'Passionately, madly!'
'But if I should turn out *not* to be a bad baronet after all, how would you love me then?'
'Madly, passionately!'
'As before?'
'Of course.'
'My darling.'

They gazed adoringly into each other's eyes. The curtain fell.

'I suppose you realize you cut six of my best lines', she said furiously.

'Did I?' he replied casually. 'Well, we can't wait all night for you to take up your bloody cue.'

At that she struck him over the head with the little string bag she carried. He turned and ran, skipping with nimble feet into the wings, and didn't stop until he had closed the door of his dressing room between him and the one whom he had once thought the most wonderful girl in the world.

'Damn', he said. 'Damn and blast!'

They had hoped to get an easy divorce in South Africa, but it didn't work out that way. For six months they played in all the big cities, living in different hotels and only meeting at the theatre. On the boat on the way home, they sat at different tables. One day he was saddened by seeing her asleep in a deckchair, looking unhappy. But what could he do about it? She would be better without him, he thought; their temperaments were entirely unsuited to each other. He became friendly with a bishop, but they did not talk about unhappy homes and divorces— it was simpler to share a beer and a joke. Yet he was stirred up enough to pray that if the divorce was not right, something would stop it.

It was December when they landed in England, and the bleak weather matched their mood. He felt unhappy, and on meeting the other woman again, realized that they were not meant for each other after all.

Only the island was left. How wonderful to get away from it all, and live in peace, surrounded by beauty and people who agreed with him.

A modest advertisement appeared in *The Times* on Friday, 9 March 1934:

> CORAL ISLAND—Gentleman owning one of the most beautiful islands on the Great Barrier Reef anxious to form small colony for poor promising boys or orphans. Would like to hear from anyone keen to take financial interest to make this possible.

This was a real life story. The *Daily Mirror* gave it

full-page treatment with these striking headlines:

SINGER AS MODERN ROBINSON CRUSOE
£500 Island in Coral Sea
Scheme for Twenty Boys to Develop Land

There was a photo of Ivan smoking a pipe and another of the island.

Many provincial papers gave great publicity to the scheme. More than a thousand letters came in from all sorts of people. It was staggering to discover how many wanted to escape to a tropical island.

A young woman called Peggy Williams saw the front page spread in the *Daily Mirror*. She was convinced she knew a better answer to life's problems than running away to a Pacific island. In spite of the amused doubts of her friends she determined to see this man and tell him so.

When they met Ivan was so intrigued by her disconcerting questions that he invited her to dinner. She asked him if he really thought he would solve anyone's problems by transporting them to a South Sea island. Had he found the answer to his own problems, and, if not, how did he propose to help those he took out with him? He forgave her directness because she was so charming about it. They talked for hours about God and how to change the world, and she invited him to an Oxford Group house party.

The Oxford Group, better known today as Moral Re-Armament, had been gaining ground rapidly in Britain, especially in Oxford University since the arrival of Dr Frank Buchman there in 1921. This had been followed by remarkable changes in the lives of many undergraduates and some of the dons. Much of its work was done through house parties which were an accepted part of English social life in the twenties. It was to one of these that Peggy Williams invited Ivan.

She had certainly made him think. She was different from most religious people whom he knew. Her faith was practical. He met some of her friends, and began to understand their basic principles. They believed that God has a plan for every man's life, and can direct anyone who takes time to listen for His guidance. It was very important, they said, to give adequate time every day, especially in the early morning, to be quiet so that God could speak and direct one's thoughts. They said they found it helpful to write such thoughts down. He wondered what sort of things God would say to him if he listened.

His new friends also said that before you can expect God to give you clear direction, you must let Him speak to you about the way you have lived so far. They summed up Christ's teaching on moral standards in four absolutes—absolute honesty, purity, unselfishness and love. Ivan didn't have to think long to know that, on that basis, some things in his life would have to change. He could see sense in what they said.

Some weeks passed before Ivan decided to make a test. He had always prayed at important times, such as when in danger during the war and before his first audition for the D'Oyly Carte Opera Company. He now prayed that God would prove to him that life could be satisfying without one of the things he had always thought essential—his pipe.

He set out on a fishing trip, having first written a

letter to God, which he left with his pipe lying on it, telling Him that he really wanted to find out whether the life his new friends talked about was possible for him. Would He please make this one day as enjoyable without his pipe as with it? To his surprise it worked. He remembers fishing in a beautiful tarn and stopping and saying aloud, 'If only I could be sure of God'. 'Suddenly', he recalls, 'everything became alive. The mountains, it seemed to me, danced. I was surrounded, enveloped by God. A compelling thought came to me to go to the house party to which Peggy Williams had invited me.'

So he arrived at Oxford. It was a beautiful mid-summer day in July 1934 and he was full of anticipation for what he thought would be a very interesting week-end, probably a few meetings interspersed with some pleasant hours punting on the river with that delightful young lady.

The first person he met was a lanky youth who introduced himself as Miles Phillimore. He was most friendly and it was not long before Ivan was rattling off his life history. He became quite eager to go along to a meeting in the Town Hall, but was determined not to be influenced by anything that seemed like mass pressure.

Ivan says: 'I especially took note when a Canadian business man and his wife said they had been on the verge of divorce and believed they could never be happy together again, but that they had found a new meaning to marriage. Each had learned, they said, to look at where he or she was at fault instead of blaming the other. There was freedom from any emotional exhibitionism which as an actor I would have scented at once. So I said to myself, "There is no doubt they have got something and they are absolutely right, but I am sure my wife would never see this". Then I thought, "Well, perhaps God may want me to be divorced. How wonderful it would be to marry a woman who was like one of these who listened to God and did not argue with me or want her own way! Yes, there is something in this. I must have a talk to someone after the meeting."

'I chose Walter Seaman, a good-looking young man with a voice that encouraged confidence. He told me how he had been released from certain problems that had bothered him. He went on to say that when he had been completely honest about himself and given his life to God, Christ had become a reality in his life. I remember thinking, "If this man can have such an experience, why not I?" It was something I wanted for myself—not just bits, all of it. I didn't much like this business of being drastically honest, but I thought if I had to stand on my head in the middle of the High Street and shout "Hallelujah" to get it, I'd do it. I would give this a try.

'So I wrote down those four absolute standards— honesty, purity, unselfishness and love—and asked God to show me a picture of what I looked like to Him, and what I might have to do or face or let go if I was to find this spiritual power which would simplify life. As thoughts came to mind I noted them down. I would have to tell my wife where I had failed her. Then there was that family in Australia whose father had threatened to shoot me if He ever saw me again because of the hurt I had caused his daughter. There was the way I told some stories so often that I began to believe they were true. And sometimes I would copy a piece of poetry and send it to a girl friend as my own composition. When I was writing a song, I would borrow a few bars to impress people with my versatility. There was a little matter of some money I had misappropriated at a theatrical garden party, and once I had changed the label on a swim-suit I was buying so that I got it cheaper.

'Well', concluded Ivan, 'I decided there was no way out. I went down on my knees and told God that was the sort of person I was (which He doubtless knew) and that it would have to be a super-miracle if I was going to be different, but I was willing to place myself at His disposal if He could use me in any way. The immediate effect was upon my own feelings. There was a relief in not having to wear a mask any more. I could be myself.

'At the meeting next morning in the Town Hall, I determined to drive in my stake straight away by telling what had happened to me. In my excitement I nearly fell over the balcony as I got up to speak. I said I felt that the curtain was going up on the greatest act of my life, and I hoped it would never come down.'

Ivan stayed at Oxford for a month because he wanted to cultivate as much of this new spiritual power as possible before seeing his wife. Finally he could wait no longer and drove down to Brighton where she was playing in 'Brighton Follies'. He had already written to tell her of his experience and that he would like to talk to her about it.

He relates, 'When I arrived, the first test of my new-found faith came when she did not want to see me, and I felt I was calling upon a complete stranger. My small daughter was there, Elsie's partner in the show and her parents. I was even less popular with them than before, if that was possible, and at dinner that night one almost needed a fur coat, the atmosphere was so frigid. Yet the miracle to me was that my heart was warm. I had a strong sense all the time that Jesus Christ was beside me. And even after Elsie's mother had taken the flowers I had brought and thrown them out of the window, and pretty well thrown me after them, I was warm and giving. I could not have done it without Christ's presence.

'Somehow or other I could never get Elsie alone to tell her the things I thought she ought to know. Then I met her on the hotel stairs one morning and there was nothing for it but to take that opportunity of talking to her, while various maids and visitors were going up and down.'

Elsie could not ignore what had happened to her husband, but the memory of how cruel his tongue could be was too painful for her to face returning to him. She said she distrusted religion. Furthermore it was probably just another of Ivan's fads and wouldn't last.

It wasn't easy for Ivan either. What should he do next? Perhaps after all divorce would be the best solution. However, to put it in his own words, 'The great thing now was to keep close to God and find out each day what He wanted me to do.'

He wasn't quite prepared for what happened next. He received an invitation to go and live in the East End of London with a friend he had met at Oxford. This man, Frank Bygott, was going to do a bit of boxing as a means of getting to know people in this part of the town, which was the home of many famous boxers and where the way to a man's heart was to put the gloves

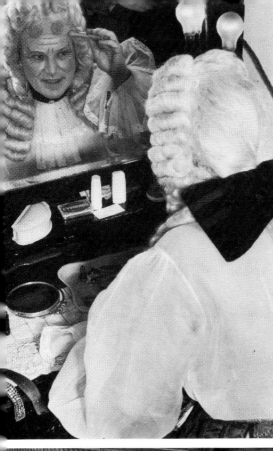

**Ivan Menzies
making up as the
Duke of Plaza
Toro in**
The Gondoliers
photo: Illustrations Ltd

**Crowds waiting
for the doors to open
when the D'Oyly
Carte Company
performed at His
Majesty's Theatre,
Perth**

One of his favourite roles was that of Jack Point
in *The Yeomen of the Guard*

on with him. Ivan's heart sank a little at the thought of dark winter months in the East End, instead of lovely sunshine on a tropical island, but he went. He didn't do any boxing, nor did he acquire a taste for jellied eels, a great delicacy in those parts. But he did begin to learn how the other half of the world lived, sometimes with seven or eight in a room.

Ivan's future was now in the melting pot. Did his new way of life mean that he had to abandon the stage? After a struggle with himself he became willing to do so, if that was what God wanted. Then came an offer of the principal comedian's part in a pantomime, *Aladdin*. He felt it right to accept, but first explained to the manager that he was associated with the Oxford Group. To his surprise, the manager replied that that was why he had approached him—he wanted a clean show.

Ivan took along with him as his dresser an unemployed dock labourer whom he had met in the East End and had brought to an experience of God. Now they could support each other. Rehearsals began and it soon became apparent that something was not right with the production. The manager asked Ivan's advice, but although he engaged two popular acts to cover what Ivan said were the weak spots, he was unable to save the pantomime. After three weeks it closed down.

Once Ivan would have been depressed and all his fears of failure would have come to the surface. Now he found his security no longer lay at the mercies of a critical public. But the problem remained: what was he to do with the next years? He had had excellent notices in the London papers, some expressing the hope that London would see more of him. He received a good offer to star in a new farce at the Adelphi, but, as he read the script, his heart sank because he realised it did not measure up to what he now stood for. In spite of offers of a still higher salary, followed by threats of being on the West End managers' black list, he had to refuse. Then he was invited by J C Williamson's to make another Australian tour with the Gilbert and Sullivan Opera Company. This offer he accepted.

4

Away, away! my heart's on fire
— The Pirates of Penzance

Ivan was eager to return to the land that had given him so much pleasure, but most of all he felt it was a call from God to pioneer in a country that had never known a major spiritual awakening. To his sorrow Elsie was unable or unwilling to accompany him, but other principals of the Company did. This was in the days before rapid air transport and he looked forward to five weeks' leisurely travel via Suez Canal.

Not long after the ship sailed from Tilbury he was passing the bar of the saloon when familiar voices called, 'Come on, Jimmy,* come and join us.' He sat down and ordered a lemonade. A deadly silence fell. One of his friends asked if there was any rule that prevented him from having a whisky and soda. 'None whatever', he replied. 'Nor is there any rule against my having a lemonade'. He had won his point. Many questions followed. What was this all about? Did it mean he would no longer tell his old stories? He told them a new one—of how he had changed. Right from the start he had decided that there was to be no hole-and-corner Christianity for him.

An officer on the way to Abyssinia alternated between scepticism and talking of his problems. Then he grew angry and spent the next three days in the bar. On the fourth day he met Ivan on the deck, and they

*Ivan was known as 'Jimmy' in the profession.

chatted a while about the weather. Presently he asked, 'Aren't you going to tick me off?'

'What on earth for?' asked Ivan.

'For being tight for three days', he replied.

Ivan answered, 'If you want to rot your liver to spite God, what's it got to do with me?'

When Easter came the chaplain asked Ivan to take the service.

'Let's do it together', Ivan said.

The ship's lounge was packed. Both chaplain and actor spoke of what Easter meant to them since they had found new life through an experience of Christ and His Cross. Many of the passengers came to talk afterwards. The next day was very rough and Ivan followed the example of the Admiral in *HMS Pinafore*

> *When the breezes blow*
> *I generally go below*
> *And seek the seclusion that the cabin grants.*

He used the opportunity to talk to the steward of his new experience.

For Ivan there was never a dull moment. His cabin mate, a Congregational minister from Adelaide, marvelled at his sparkle.

'All on water', said Ivan with a twinkle.

Reports that Jimmy had 'gone all religious' had reached the Directors of the Company in Australia and perturbed them. On arrival he was met at the ship by one of them, who greeted him with the words, 'Hullo, Jimmy, have you brought your Bible?'

'I certainly have', he replied, pulling out a pocket edition of Moffatt's New Testament along with his Gilbert and Sullivan libretto.

'It's the new book of words as far as I'm concerned', he declared with a smile.

The Director felt uneasy and Ivan impulsively offered to tear up his contract. However, he advised the Director to wait and see what happened before accepting the offer.

The Press appreciated the story and it appeared in both evening and morning papers. One of the leading dailies asked him to write about his experiences, and this caused considerable interest. Soon the Oxford Group and Ivan Menzies were to become as inseparable in the minds of Australians as Marco and Guiseppe in *The Gondoliers*.

The old securities in which men had trusted were crumbling. The Great Depression had reached a point where one in three Australian workers was unemployed. Men tramped the streets in a desperate search for work, or waited with a sense of shame in long queues to receive their relief rations. As the country struggled towards renewed prosperity, the emergence of Hitler and Mussolini in Europe gave fresh cause for concern. The ineffectiveness of the League of Nations destroyed confidence in collective security. Yet young people still believed it was possible to 'shake the silly old world into place'.* Many were to respond hopefully to Ivan Menzies and the changes he began to bring about in individuals in those formative years had a profound effect on Australia and New Zealand.

The Gilbert and Sullivan tour in 1935 began with a short season in Adelaide, the capital of South Australia. That was when we, the authors, first met Ivan Menzies.

*Brennan, Niall: Dr Mannix (Rigby, Adelaide, 1964) p249

We were a very ordinary couple, going quietly about our work as secondary school teacher and housewife, unaware of the fireball that was soon to explode.

We had both read A J Russell's best-seller about the Group, *For Sinners Only*, in the year before we were married, and had found a new reality in our Christian experience. Others joined us and we arranged a house party.

Just before it was due to begin the evening paper announced that Ivan Menzies had arrived in Australia for three purposes: first, to play as principal comedian in the Gilbert and Sullivan Opera Company; secondly, to inspect an island in the Pacific which he had bought; and thirdly, to start the Oxford Group in Australia.

At last someone had arrived who apparently knew all about the Oxford Group!

Ivan agreed to meet those planning the house-party. 'I take it', he began, 'that I'm talking to people who know what change means?' Everyone nodded complacently. He then asked what the purpose of the house-party was. Did we have an answer for a man such as he had been?

'The last time I was in Adelaide', he said, 'I nearly ended up in gaol for holding beer parties behind the Zoo. If a drunk comes into your meeting, have you got a changed drunk in your team to give him the answer to his problem?'

No, we had all been respectable church-going people.

'Well', said Ivan, 'You've still got a fortnight. Get out and change your drunk.'

One young man objected to these outrageous questions, protesting that we were not an *Oxford* Group.

'I don't care whether you are an Oxford Group or a Timbuctoo Group', Ivan retorted. 'Are you changing lives?'

'How long do you spend each morning in quiet, listening to God?' he asked next — 'one hour? two hours? three hours?'

We were left in no doubt that the kind of Oxford Group Ivan talked about was very different from our cosy fellowship. We were being challenged to a revolutionary way of life and we'd have to do something about it. At least one man who had been eager to meet the famous Ivan Menzies slipped away quickly in case Ivan Menzies wanted to meet him. Most of us stood in little groups at street corners or front gates talking late into the night. We had caught a tiger by the tail. What were we to do next?

Special afternoon tea parties had been arranged by a leading department store at which principals of the Gilbert and Sullivan Opera Company appeared as speakers. When Ivan Menzies was advertised as the guest speaker, a large crowd of fashionable women came, ready to be amused by the famous comedian. Cigarette smoke drifted through the restaurant; the chatter of women's voices grew louder; then above it was heard the penetrating voice of a man. Ivan had arrived. He threaded his way through the crowded tables, talking all the time with a continuous patter of funny stories, until he reached the platform.

He began by talking about his favourite role, that of Jack Point in *The Yeoman of the Guard*. He observed how the jester really died of self-pity.

'But', he continued, 'when the curtain went down

Jack Point had to get up and go on with life. One doesn't die of self-pity in real life.'

He went on to say that even the exciting life of a popular comedian had come to seem empty and meaningless, until one day the curtain went up on the greatest act of his life—when he decided to let God take control. A hush came over the audience; one could have heard a pin drop. Ivan seemed blissfully unaware that he was doing anything unusual.

He was certainly causing a stir. He had agreed to come to the Sunday evening church service with which our house-party was to end. Cliff was to be one of the speakers but felt uncomfortable about speaking with such a vital person in the congregation, so withdrew.

On the Saturday afternoon the first session began. To our amazement, a young police-cadet friend of ours, whom we had been trying unsuccessfully to convert in the orthodox way, came along and offered to help in any way he could. We gathered that he had seen Ivan and something remarkable had happened. We paced the streets asking ourselves what were the implications of all this for us. Dare we respond to the bigger challenge that Ivan was bringing?

Later that evening we discussed whether to go and see Ivan at the theatre and have a talk. 'At any rate', said Cliff, 'I don't suppose it will do any harm.'

We got there just as the show was ending. Despite the fact that Ivan had given two performances that day, he received us in his dressing room. As we entered somewhat nervously, we noticed several copies of the New Testament lying among the grease paints. No time was wasted in preliminary civilities.

'How do you face up to the four absolute moral standards?' was his first question.

'Oh, pretty well', Edna replied. 'I've been to church all my life.'

'So you think you are perfect?' he retorted.

Turning to Cliff, he asked, 'Does your wife know all about you?'

The fact was that she knew very little, and might as well have been married to a clam. Then Ivan talked rapidly for some time about what he understood revolutionary living to be. At about midnight his face lit up with that flashing smile that endears him even to those whom he has been treating rather roughly, and said, 'I'm meeting another couple at eleven o'clock tomorrow morning at my hotel. If you want to go on with this, come and join us.'

The last trams had departed by now and taxis were too expensive for us, so we walked the two or three miles home. The clam began to open and we talked to each other of many things never before brought to light.

Next morning when we called at the hotel the other couple turned out to be the police-cadet friend and his fiancée, who was Edna's cousin and had been her bridesmaid. We nearly fell on each other's necks.

Ivan told us that he had been invited to speak at the Sunday church service. He did not realise that Cliff had previously been asked and withdrawn.

'It looks as though God has sent a team, so off we go!' he said cheerfully.

That evening, after the service, Ivan spoke and then introduced us. Now we had something to say. We shared our fresh experience in front of the eight hundred people present. The police-cadet spoke of the thirty-nine letters of restitution he had to write that weekend. For instance, he had climbed over a fence instead of paying to go through the gate at football matches, and had now forwarded the money he owed. There were so many similar letters that he had run out of money and could only make promises of payment. This cadet, Ray Whitrod, is now Commissioner of Police in the state of Queensland, after having been Commissioner of the Commonwealth and the Papua-New Guinea Forces. He told us recently that the absolute standards Ivan had put before him had given him something basic for his work and that he regards them as essential for making value judgements.

5

No half-and-half affair, I mean
— The Gondoliers

The next day the Company left Adelaide for Melbourne. Ivan had never played to a more enthusiastic audience than the one that filled Her Majesty's Theatre on the opening night, and he gave what he knew was his best performance so far. In his curtain speech he said he was happy to be able to give his audience not only a few hours' entertainment but also something that could help solve the problems of the country.

The Directors were delighted at the reception given to the Company but still had serious doubts about this injection of religion into the theatre, and made attempts to dissuade him from it. In all his curtain speeches he continued to refer to the Oxford Group. One of the principals threatened to leave the Company if he continued doing so. Ivan at first took the attitude, 'Too bad. Leave if you like but I'll stay and go on with my speeches', but when one of the Directors, possibly as a kind of bribe, offered him the use of the theatre at any time for an Oxford Group meeting, if he would make no more references to it from the stage, he realized that he had been trying to move too fast. In his enthusiasm he was causing hostility within the Company, and rousing more public interest than he could deal with, so he decided to move more slowly until he had gathered a stronger force of men and women to support him. For some time he ceased to use the theatre as his platform, and when he did so again it was with the approval of the management.

Soon he was inundated with requests to speak to various clubs and institutions, and a stream of visitors was coming to his dressing room at the theatre and his sitting room in Menzies Hotel. The management and staff of the hotel were very co-operative, especially after one of the waiters made restitution to the manager concerning the theft of wines over a long period. Through his contact with Ivan the manager gained a new Christian faith and became an official of his church.

Ivan's unconventional behaviour must at times have astounded the more conservative. He was asked to open a new dance club organized by some of the bright young set of Melbourne. He arrived in a white tie and tails, and was taken to the centre of the floor with the young folk gathered around him. For twenty minutes he talked to an intent group about what Christ had done for him, and suggested that if they ran the club in the way God wanted they would both get the greatest happiness out of it and also give something to other young people which could affect the whole country. He then declared the club open, and those who were not too dazed began to dance. Some gathered round his table and spent the evening talking.

Church leaders were puzzled by this unusual evange-list who proclaimed his message with strong conviction but in odd places and with what seemed an irreverent hilarity. Some criticized, while others sought him out, hoping that their own spirits might be refreshed. Many invited him to speak to their congregations.

He had been brought up by his mother to go to church every Sunday morning but it had failed to grip his imagination. He said later, 'I thought the Church was a good show, badly produced by poor actors. So I cut it out.'

The first man he went to see when he went home to his village after the Oxford house-party was the vicar, whom he had often ridiculed. 'If I acted like he preached', Ivan had said, 'I'd be hit with a bottle.'

The vicar must have wondered what had prompted this rare visit. Ivan apologised for his past attitude of destructive criticism. The Church, he told the astonished vicar, could be a force that would save humanity if critics like himself put their energy into constructive action, and that was what he intended to do.

A youth leader in the village had felt very much the same as Ivan had about the Church. Ivan told him of his discoveries and he began to share the same experience. The first Sunday morning on which Ivan went to early Communion was very wet, and the only two communicants besides the sexton and the vicar were this young man and himself. He could not resist pointing out to the vicar that whatever he thought about his methods, at least it had doubled the number of his communicants that Sunday!

The Church, Ivan believed, should be proclaiming the message of Christ with a trumpet call that had an unmistakable sound. In Australia, as he was given the opportunity, he put this challenge sometimes from a cathedral pulpit, to a gathering of clergymen, or in a heart-to-heart talk with an individual seeking the way to a more effective ministry.

A service at which Ivan Menzies preached was a stirring experience. Church-goers who join in the martial strains of 'Onward Christian Soldiers' may not be aware that the popular tune is the work of Sir Arthur Sullivan. It was not simply for this reason that Ivan Menzies so often concluded with this hymn. He had a vision for the Church as it was meant to be, and the hymn expressed it so well:

> *Like a mighty army*
> *Moves the Church of God.*

One very wet night he was preaching in Brisbane cathedral. Despite the rain the cathedral was packed, and the actor responded to the full house. After a stirring address he announced the closing hymn, his usual 'Onward, Christian Soldiers'.

'Like a mighty army moves the Church of God', he cried. 'When we get to that part let's really lift the roof off and let the whole city know that a spiritual revolution has started here.' The organist, who was notorious for the loudness of his playing, pulled out all the stops and the cathedral rafters shook. Then, alas, the organ broke down completely. The last verse had to be sung unaccompanied and the slightly deflated preacher walked down the aisle in silence. In the vestry later the Dean remarked, 'Well, Mr Menzies, I must congratulate you on creating two records tonight. You have filled the cathedral on a wet night, and you have succeeded in silencing our organist.'

Scores of Christian ministers found something new in their experience through meeting Ivan Menzies. His challenge was direct and penetrating. Take no one for granted, was his motto.

Like the court jester of old, Ivan used a comedian's privilege to make his barbed remarks in a humorous way that rendered them more acceptable. A Melbourne clergyman, the Rev Eric Kent, once told him that in their earlier years he and his wife had intended to go to Japan as missionaries. Ivan looked at them with a smile, and commented, 'Oh, the poor Japanese'; then added, 'Why don't you start to get yourselves right first?' That's what they did. Ivan remarked to him a few years later, 'You know, Eric, when I first met you, you were the finest-looking parson for a funeral that I had ever met.'

One of Australia's best-known clergymen, the Rev Dr (now Sir) Irving Benson, tells of the remarkable influence Ivan Menzies had upon him. Dr Benson relates how at an unusually early age he had come to the 'Cathedral Church' of his denomination, Wesley Church, Melbourne, where he supervised the Central Methodist Mission and preached every week to one of the largest congregations in Australia, with thousands more listening on the radio. He was successful—one could say famous—throughout Australia. Conversions occurred regularly in his church. People came to see him frequently for spiritual counsel. Yet, looking at the post-war world, he felt a sense of frustration. The League of Nations was proving ineffective for want of spiritual support. The economic Depression and the cruel unemployment that came with it made him sick at heart. 'How could the world ever realise the Kingdom of God?' he asked himself. 'I could scarcely bear to think about it.'

Then he heard of what Ivan Menzies was doing in

Melbourne. 'He won men and women in the University, his fellow-actors, doctors, solicitors, society women and the most unlikely people. What he accomplished reminds me of Paul entering a strange city and, by witnessing to first one and then another, forming a Christian group, each member a vital witness. Here was the Book of Acts in action.

'I opened my pulpit to this wonderful little man, this radiant Christian, and he spoke over the air to the Australian continent. The response was an avalanche of appeals—men and women in and out of the Church crying for what he had experienced. I gathered the ministers of all Churches together and turned Ivan Menzies loose upon us.'

In the week following the editor of the official Methodist journal devoted his leading article to Ivan Menzies. 'In him', the editor wrote, 'all were forced to recognise a disarming frankness, simplicity and earnestness. Ivan Menzies, all unconsciously brought his hearers face to face with God and with elemental truth.' *

Dr Benson had many intimate talks with Ivan. Although one of Australia's greatest preachers, he was humble enough to learn from a comedian.

One afternoon the two men drove out together.

'Are you absolutely surrendered to God?' asked Ivan, as they talked.

'Yes, I can truthfully say that I have no ambition in this world but to do the will of God.'

A more searching question followed.

'Do you absolutely surrender to God every day?'

'I have not consciously done so', was the reply.

*The Spectator and Methodist Chronicle, 21 August 1935

Ivan spoke of what daily surrender had done for him and went on to talk about the work of life-changing. Dr Benson said that he had constantly been used in bringing men and women to Christ. Ivan asked if they in turn brought others to the same experience. He explained how important this outreach is, 'for this is the only way we can get God's plan working in the world.'

'I saw it', says Sir Irving, 'I humbly and gratefully saw it all....Daily checking on the "four absolutes" revealed to me things I had never questioned in myself....

'Now my world sickness had gone—I knew how the world could be changed. Evil social and international conditions always are everywhere caused through individual evil lives. When individuals' lives are changed and brought together into groups—these groups are fellowships of reconciliation through which Christ can work.' *

Whenever Ivan was advertised to speak, crowds gathered. What brought them? One young woman from Adelaide, Pat Salter (now Mrs George Wood) says she was startled by the phenomenon of a popular comedian preaching in St Peter's Cathedral.

There was a touch of the theatrical in his entry, Mrs Wood remembers, as he went bobbing down the aisle in surplice and cassock behind the mitred figure of the Bishop, bowing to his 'audience' right and left as he proceeded. All the world's a stage, he seemed to think, even an Anglican cathedral. One who was present recalls the opening with which he captured attention.

'Who has read the nineteenth chapter of St Mark's Gospel lately?' he enquired innocently.

*Benson, C Irving: *The Eight Points of the Oxford Group* OUP 1938 pp143—150

Hands went up in many places.

'Now I feel thoroughly at home', he said. 'There is no nineteenth chapter of Mark.'

One lady who had been tricked into putting her hand up wrote him an indignant letter a few days later. Her friends, she complained, were all stopping her in the street and asking whether she had read the nineteenth chapter of Mark that morning. Ivan replied that the best thing she could do was to tell them what was in the other sixteen.

In Perth, Western Australia, Archbishop Le Fanu, Primate of Australia, had lunch with Ivan and asked him to speak in the cathedral. The verger packed the crowd in, and as he found space for the last two to squeeze in, he realised he could not get in himself and had to go across the street and listen to the service on a friend's radio.

Many of the church services at which Ivan spoke were broadcast. (Television was still many years ahead.) A heavy postbag usually resulted. One letter came from a boundary rider far out in the bush, who said he had to ride many miles alone every day, and he used to wonder whether there was a God. He understood many things more clearly now, he wrote, as this talk had come from a man who did not preach to him but shared his experiences.

A business man came to see Ivan after a broadcast. He had been suffering from a bad hangover and had just had a quarrel with his wife when something made him switch on the radio. Ivan's words hit him hard. His interest was held for the rest of the talk, and at the end of it he went down on his knees and gave his life to God. His home, which had been close to breaking up, was remade.

Ivan found that there was not always time to deal adequately with the deep issues in the lives of those he met, but he had the art of saying the thing that at least set them on a new path.

One evening an unemployed man met Ivan at the stage door and wanted to borrow ten shillings. He asked the man to come back at the end of the show and have supper with him at the restaurant next door. Meanwhile, he could sit in the park and read a book written by one of Ivan's friends.* He was waiting at the end of the performance, and said no man could live up to that book and he was contemplating throwing himself into the harbour. Ivan said, 'Well, let's go and have some food first while I tell you about a better solution, and if this doesn't work after you have tried it, I'll go into the harbour with you.'

Over the meal Ivan told his own story, and using the paper serviette, the man began to write down some of the first steps he would have to take. They included going to a certain hotel out of which he had walked without paying his bill, owning up and promising to pay as soon as he could. He missed getting a job because he was honest about himself, but two days later he got a better one and set about paying off his debts. He was a Roman Catholic, and went immediately to his priest to confess what a bad Catholic he had been and to declare that he now intended to be better.

*Kitchen, V C: *I was a Pagan* Hodder and Stoughton, 1934

6

Though you have surely strayed,
Take heart of grace,
Your step retrace
  — The Pirates of Penzance

On 19 June 1937, an article appeared on the front page of the Melbourne *Truth* headed 'Comedian started Oxford Group in gaol'. Although the writer appeared only half-serious it became clear that something unusual had been happening within the prison walls, and a prominent Penal Department official was quoted as saying of certain prisoners: 'Whatever the reason, all fourteen, since joining the Oxford Group, are changed men. Reports from overseers of workshops are excellent concerning them'. What, then, was it all about?

It began one evening as Ivan was dashing in the Stage Door after a very busy day. A gentleman in a clerical collar stopped him and introduced himself as the chaplain of Melbourne's big Pentridge Gaol. A man there, he said, was serving a life sentence for murder. He particularly wanted Ivan to see this prisoner because he was the unhappiest man in the gaol and he himself had had no effect upon him. Ivan's first feeling was that he would rather talk to the chaplain and try to show him how to make a new approach. He felt, however, that it was right to go to the prison as requested. Rising before five o'clock on the following Sunday morning to allow adequate time for God's guidance, he arrived at the prison in time for their seven o'clock service, at which he had promised to speak. He was to see the murderer later.

Speaking in a prison chapel, especially at that time on a Sunday morning when all good actors were just going to bed, was a new experience for Ivan. He began by playing the organ and singing them a comic song. An eager, hungry look came into the faces of many of the prisoners as he began his talk.

The governor of the prison gave all the help he could, offering to pick out a few men who were really keen to go further and to arrange for Ivan to meet them in his own room on the following Sunday.

During the week he had the chance to meet the man the chaplain wanted him to see. As the prisoner told the story of his crime, Ivan was silently praying for the right thing to say. 'I too am a murderer', he said quietly. The startled man's eyes opened wide. 'How did you get away with it?' he wanted to know. Ivan explained that he had kept his 'murders' within the law. His favourite weapon was an unbridled tongue that wrought havoc and often 'murdered' the feelings of his wife and others. He also harboured resentment and hatred in his heart at times, and according to Christ's Sermon on the Mount these feelings made him a murderer in his heart.

The man was now listening intently. When his unusual visitor told him of other things which had shut him off from God, he said no one had ever talked to him like that before. What seemed to make the strongest appeal was the puzzling fact that a popular idol, who could quite easily have taken whatever he wanted from life gave his time to come and talk to a man like him. Ivan told him that he had nothing to lose by making the same experiment as he had made. By now he was so desperate to find a way out of the abyss into which he had sunk that he confessed several things he had not told the authorities, and declared that he was ready to do whatever God asked of him concerning them. He went down on his knees and gave his life to God. He rose, with a sense of lightness as though a heavy load had rolled off him.

When Ivan returned on the following Sunday to meet the little group of men chosen by the governor, he had a good team-mate in this 'changed' murderer, who had already been telling others about his new experience. The governor, thinking that his presence might cramp the men, left Ivan alone with them—a murderer, another man serving a life sentence for shooting a bank manager, one doing a long term for theft on ships, and another with many years for forgery. The thief used to go on fashionable pleasure cruises, and mingle with the drinkers in the bar; then he would help the drunken ones to their cabins, and reward himself for his helpfulness by removing a few notes from their wallets. Next morning he would go to them and sympathize with them for having spent so much in the bar. Ivan tried to show these men something that made shooting bank managers, forging bank notes, or stealing from drunken tourists seem just too dull for words.

Regular visits to Pentridge were continued for some time, Ivan often taking friends to back him up. One by one prisoners changed until the group numbered fourteen. Some of them wrote to Ivan about their experience.

J M, after twenty years as a burglar and receiver of stolen goods, considered himself an expert in tricking society out of 'easy money'. He was not quite expert enough. In 1936 he was doing a second sentence in Pentridge, this time four and a half years' hard labour. 'I am still here', he wrote, 'and shall be for eight months, but here is the difference. Having surrendered my life to God, I have found a new joy.'

He went on to write of the change in one of his mates. This man he described as one from whom 'any talk of religion brought forth a torrent of abuse'. Yet when he was finally persuaded to come to a meeting he got such a shock that 'the result is a new man for Christ'. His letter ended with a sentence that Ivan treasures, 'Be sure that the prayers of a grateful bunch of chaps go with you from Pentridge prison.'

The task of building men up in a new-found faith demands sustained care, and Ivan's aim was that, by the time for their release, these prisoners would be mature enough to stand alone and go straight. Where possible he kept touch with them after their release. It was not always easy because crime was so deeply ingrained in some of them that they had come to look on it as the normal means of earning a living.

There is a sequel to the Pentridge story. Five years later, when Ivan addressed the directors of a certain club in Melbourne, one of them stood up and, introducing himself as a former Commissioner of Police, told the story of one of his policemen. This man's home had broken up and he was divorced. Shortly afterwards he was convicted of an offence which landed him in Pentridge prison at the time when Ivan Menzies' influence there was spreading. As a result he was changed. On his release from prison he remarried his former wife, and shortly afterwards was appointed to a position of trust in the city.

Another prisoner who made good was 'Robbie', the 'tough guy' of the prison at the time Ivan Menzies came there. If he objected to an order given by a warder, he was likely to bash the man's face, and was often confined to his cell for refractory conduct. Ivan's approach was to tell him that one day he would have to face a greater Judge than the one who had sentenced him. He did not appear to accept the full challenge that Ivan gave him, but there was such a difference in him that he was released early for good conduct and his influence on other prisoners.

The next time Ivan came to Melbourne some years later he invited Robbie to supper. 'You don't want to be seen with a crook', Robbie at first protested, but he came. By now he was in a good job. It was wartime, and one day Ivan received a letter from Colonel X, General MacArthur's ADC, stating that Robbie had applied to join the American Intelligence and had given his name as a reference. Ivan replied that he had confidence in the man, but warned that he needed to be carefully handled. Some years later, when Ivan was crossing the Atlantic by ship he spoke at a church service. A man came up afterwards and introdced himself as Colonel X, the ADC who had inquired about Robbie. Ivan asked how he had turned out.

'He was one of the finest men we ever had in Intelligence', the Colonel replied.

7

With courage rare and resolution manly
— The Pirates of Penzance

The Company moved on to Sydney, the oldest and largest city in Australia. Ivan's old Cossack dresser who had known him in the earlier days was amazed at the difference in him and convinced that only God could have brought this about. He became an ally. One evening a young lady who had known the old Ivan of the previous tour dashed into the dressing-room crying 'Darling' and was about to throw her arms around his neck when the dresser came forward with a book, saying politely, 'Excuse me, Mr Menzies him much changed now. Pardon, have you read this book *For Sinners Only*? It is very good. I have read it and am changed too.' It was so unexpected but done so artlessly that the astonished young lady could not be offended.

One of the cleaners in the theatre had been reading some of the booklets displayed on Ivan's miniature bookstall. She wanted to know whether God could speak to *her*, and was encouraged to make the experiment of listening. The next night there was a note on the table telling him she had done so and was very happy because of it. A few people began to meet in the dressing-room for a time of quiet before the curtain went up. The power of God was apparent in what happened to those who came to that room after the curtain fell.

A highlight of the time in Sydney was a party Ivan

gave one night on the stage. While the scenery was being cleared away at the end of *Ruddigore* and the stage was being set for supper, three to four hundred guests sat in the stalls while Ivan and his team spoke to them from one of the boxes. Among the speakers was a well-known actress, Maud Jeffries. She said that she had been so unhappy that there was never a night she went to bed without wishing she would die before the morning, but after hearing Ivan, from her own profession, speak publicly of his experience of Christ she had come to a similar experience. The last Christmas was the happiest she had ever known.

When the guests sat down to supper they completely filled the stage. A journalist came to Ivan and said, 'This is a miracle I never dreamt I should see. Here are about four hundred people who sat like mice for an hour after the curtain had fallen and listened to people talking about God.' 'The sound of laughter and merriment almost drowns my voice as I speak to you', he added, 'yet there is not an alcoholic drink on the table and everybody seems happy. What is the secret?'

The Gilbert and Sullivan season in Sydney was long enough for the chain reaction of Ivan's life-changing to begin to be seen. The Head Deaconess from the Anglican Cathedral came to see him and found a new dimension to her faith; through her a young nurse in one of the hospitals was changed. She had been a friend of the Premier's daughter while at the university and had stolen from her a gold fountain pen which had belonged to the Premier's mother. Now she realised that she must be honest about it, painful though that was. She wrote to the Premier (Sir Bertram Stevens) and returned the pen, telling him why. She promised to have the initials, which she had erased from the pen, re-engraved, and said she was prepared to face any consequences.

That night the Premier came to the theatre. After hearing Ivan's speech at the fall of the curtain, he came to see him, saying that he had never expected to hear such a challenge given in the theatre. He told Ivan the story of the pen and said this was evidence of the practical outreach of the ideas he was spreading. Later he met Dr Frank Buchman and told him about the fountain pen and the curtain speech, and the challenge they were to him to rise to a new level of Christian thinking.

Evelyn Gardiner, the principal contralto, found Ivan was more willing to help than formerly, as though he had grown to understand that there were others in life besides himself. 'The constantly ailing, dissipated man', she says, 'whose complexion seemed always that of a bilious child, and whose eyes were dull, is now never sick, a spruce well-groomed man with a bright eye, who rises early and has energy all day long—meeting people, talking, writing and generally bringing his message to the countless millions who need encouragement.' A generous tribute from Evelyn Gardiner, since Ivan still annoyed her intensely at times! Lady Tait, who as Viola Wilson became the leading soprano for the wartime tour, reveals this in her history of the Taits and J C Williamson.* She recalls that when Eve Gardiner was singing he would sometimes mimic her perfectly and upset her so that she forgot her lines. With eyes flashing angrily she would sweep into the dressing room

*Tait, Viola: *A Family of Brothers* (Heinemann, Melbourne 1971), p152

muttering, 'That wretched little man did it again.'

Lady Tait's own memories of playing as the leading soprano opposite Ivan Menzies were pleasant. 'The one bright spot in the midst of all the war news from home was working with Ivan Menzies', she wrote. 'His wit was infectious and his clowning both on the stage and at rehearsals often had us laughing at the wrong time.' She especially enjoyed the duet 'Poor little man, poor little maid' between Rose Maybud and Robin Oakapple in *Ruddigore*, in which they drew the best from each other. Her only criticism was of his unwillingness to return with her for an encore if he did not feel like doing so. He loved applause for himself and it might have been expected, she thought, that he would have been readier to allow his partner her full share of it.

There was a freshness about his acting that she enjoyed. He was never set in his interpretation of a part, but played as he felt at the time; consequently his performance was different every night. The sincerity of his playing of Jack Point always moved her (as Elsie Maynard) so genuinely that the pathetic appeal in the eyes of the broken-hearted jester sent a shiver down her spine, and she hated deserting the little man to go off with Fairfax.

The Stage Manager admits that he undertook the second tour 'not caring too much for a repeat of Jimmy Menzies'. He had heard rumours that made him laugh. Jimmy reading the Bible! He met Jimmy on his arrival in Australia and was puzzled. It was the same Jimmy— but not the same Jimmy. Whereas he had been restless, his moods changing like the tides of the ocean, he seemed now to have found something satisfying. In his greeting, 'Hullo, Dick, I'm glad you're still here,' there was warmth and sincerity. As time passed, the change became more noticeable. The Stage Manager became convinced of Ivan's sincerity and saw that it was this that attracted people. Complaints still came to him, though less often, and when occasionally it was necessary to speak to Jimmy about some breach of stage etiquette, he found him easier to handle.

A crisis arose one day at a rehearsal for *Lilac Time*, which the J C Williamson Company was preparing to put on in Perth. At first it had been thought that there was no suitable player for the part of Schubert, and when some of the Company proposed Ivan Menzies the management doubted whether it was wise for a comedian to appear in a serious part. They argued that his reputation was so well established that the audience would laugh at him in whatever part he played. Ivan, however, was sure that he should play this role. No one laughed, he said, when he played Jack Point's tragedy in *The Yeomen of the Guard* because he had convinced them that he was serious; and he argued that Schubert was not a great singer, and what he himself lacked in the singing, he could compensate for in his acting and in the parts that were 'musical dialogue'. He even staggered the management by offering to underwrite any loss on the production, and they agreed that he should play the part of Schubert.

The rehearsal that morning was going badly, and one of the cast made an angry attack on Ivan for holding it up through not knowing his part. They all held their breath, remembering the old days when a situation like this would have caused a violent display of 'temperament' and the lordly challenge, 'One of us must leave the Company', knowing well that he would not be the one. This time he held his temper in check for a minute of quiet thought, and apologised for his failure. After that the rehearsal went smoothly, and *Lilac Time* was a success.

Ivan knew the power of honest apology, but did not always come so quickly to the point of being willing to say he was sorry. One night the leading lady was upset—quite unreasonably, he thought. He could see that he was to blame for some little thing that led to other things that had built up to an explosion, but jibbed at admitting his fault.

'I'm hanged if I'll apologise for my bit', he said to himself. 'It was so unnecessary for her to behave in that way.'

He felt unhappy and irritable as the inner struggle went on, until he prayed and won the victory over his pride and resentment. When he apologised, the leading lady apologised in turn and expressed her gratitude, 'I'm so glad you did that. It makes it so easy to work with you.'

Noticing one night that one of the principals was looking annoyed, Ivan inquired what was wrong and got an angry challenge: 'Is it right for you to get laughs on my lines?' He would not say in which particular lines Ivan had offended, claiming it was up to him to find out. A slightly puzzled Ivan apologised for upsetting him and declared that he would not allow a few laughs to come between them and destroy the friendly spirit that existed in the Company. To be on the safe side, Ivan cut out any laugh that had the slightest possibility of upsetting him. Later in the evening he came and shook hands, with the suggestion that Ivan should put back certain laughs which he thought were too good to leave out! It was things like these that created an unusually good spirit in the Company, so that the Stage Manager could say that the tour was one of the happiest he had ever had.

The change in Ivan Menzies' behaviour on the stage noticeably affected the quality of his performance. The theatre critic of the Brisbane *Telegraph* (15 March 1937) in discussing his portrayal of Ko-Ko in *The Mikado* analysed his artistic development: 'There was a time', he wrote, 'when Mr Menzies offended against the fundamental principles of Savoy tradition in the playing of this role. He forgot that a Gilbert and Sullivan comedian can be far too funny to be good. But today there is a subtly different Ko-Ko. The comedian must know the art of subordination. Anything that leads to a division of the audience's interest, be it comic or otherwise, by any member of the Company who by reason of the action has no spotlight upon them is bad. It is true that Mr Menzies on Saturday evening did a great many things that were funny. He did them neatly and in a funny way. And if we examine his funny "sessions" we will find that they do not occur at any times other than when the spotlight is upon him and he has the centre of the stage. That is the fundamental difference between his Ko-Ko of two or three years ago and his Ko-Ko today.'

On the final night of the Gilbert and Sullivan season in Brisbane, one of the Directors of the Company, Mr E J Tait, spoke from the stage. Linking his arm with

Ivan's, he said that he had been worried when he heard that Ivan Menzies had got involved in religion, but the Company had had a record season following the difficult years of the Depression.

'So you feel that God is practical in the theatre?' Ivan asked, and the Director agreed with a hearty, 'I'll say'.

8

The darkness has passed,
And it's daylight at last
  —Iolanthe

One shadow still hung over Ivan in the land of sunshine. Elsie was not with him. When he had left England she was sceptical about the depth of his change and how long it would last. The tour of Australia and New Zealand had been long enough for him to prove to the Company that he really was different, and now that he was returning to England he hoped to be able to convince his wife too. He arrived back in London in time to find the streets decorated and the flags flying for the coronation of King George VI in May 1937. He found Elsie more friendly than when he had left, possibly as a result of his regular letters. She had furnished a room for him in the home of a friend with whom she was living, but was still not willing to go along with his new ideas.

When Elsie went to play in Brighton for a while Ivan took a room there so that he could see more of her. He did not make much progress with her but got much closer to his seven-year-old daughter Mahala. He told her that when he sat quietly and listened to God and did what He said, his work was easier and his play more fun. To his surprise Mahala, who usually did not respond to Dad's suggestions, was ready to try listening with him. After a minute or two she said, 'God says I must say my prayers. I mustn't be so fussy about my

63

eating. I must do what my mother and grandparents tell me. Now I can go and play in the garden.'

One morning after they had been listening together, she said, 'God says that if I'm a good girl I can go up to the Lake District with you at the end of the week.' Now this presented a difficulty, as Elsie didn't want to go and wasn't eager for Mahala to go and see her grandparents without her. Her reaction was, 'There you are, I told you she would take advantage of this guidance business. She is an impressionable child.'

Ivan pointed out that Mahala's earlier thoughts in quiet times had all been good ones, but added that he certainly didn't want to force his ideas on them. He almost hoped that Mahala would not be good! But she was, amazingly so, and when the end of the week came no more opposition was voiced. Father and daughter had wonderful fun travelling together. Mahala ate whatever was put in front of her.

Later Ivan followed Elsie to Aberdeen where she was playing in a show. They drove through the snow to Braemar, and some of the ice around Elsie's heart began to thaw. They even got so far as discussing a new home together, although she was still not sure he was a man who could be lived with. She returned to London alone but was quite willing to go driving to Devon and Cornwall at Easter. They took Mahala with them and had a delightful time. The Town Clerk of St Ives, Jack Atherton, and his wife invited the family to stay with them. Their homeliness and caring convinced Elsie a little more. After three or four days there they wandered through various villages and places of interest, especially old churches. Mahala insisted on their signing every visitor's book. All three were thoroughly enjoying themselves by now and Ivan was sorry when the time came to leave the other two in Bristol with Elsie's parents, who had cared for Mahala most of the time since the break-up of the marriage.

The next move came in the August holidays when friends offered the Menzies family the loan of their home near the sea front at Bournemouth. Although nothing was said both Ivan and Elsie looked on this as an experiment to see whether it was possible for them to live together again. When Elsie saw that Ivan made no demands on her, she relaxed and started enjoying looking after them both. They had a happy four weeks, and Ivan says he learnt a new way of living in marriage. In the old days Elsie had dared to mention a friend of hers whose husband lit the fire and brought her an early morning cup of tea. 'What a pansy', said Ivan. 'No woman would ever get me to do that.' Now he found himself lighting the fire and taking Elsie a cup of tea.

Elsie returned to London and Ivan spent some time in Edinburgh.

In 1938, with the threat of war looming and nations hastily rearming, Dr Buchman saw the even more urgent need for moral and spiritual rearmament on a world scale. He initiated a programme which was taken up by leaders of British life. A remarkable correspondence appeared in *The Times* and soon leaders of other countries began to urge its necessity.

The first World Assembly for Moral Re-Armament (MRA) was held in Interlaken, Switzerland, in September 1938. Ivan and Ellsie were gradually drawing closer together, and when Ivan invited Elsie and Mahala to go to Interlaken with him, she responded to the idea. She began to meet people from all over the world and enjoyed their company. She found herself making suggestions and going to the meetings. On the last night a Scot asked Elsie and Ivan whether they had listened to God together yet. Ivan inwardly panicked, remembering the reaction when he had suggested it earlier. But Elsie agreed, and they prayed together for the first time ever, and she promised to get up early with him next morning. When the first rays of sunshine were reflected off the snow-covered Jungfrau, Ivan went along the verandah to Elsie's room. Mahala's interest in quiet times had waned a little by now and she said, 'Oh, we don't have them, do we, Mummy?' but this time Elsie said, 'Yes, we do.' So all three listened together for the first time. It was fifteen months since Ivan's return from Australia. He had a deep sense of gratitude for the way God had led them.

Elsie was beginning to relent towards him, and to consider the possibility of trying to re-establish a home. Clearly he was different. He had begun to be aware of her as a person to be considered. She remembered her marriage vows. They had been taken seriously and should not be lightly put aside. The prospect of being alone in the world as she grew older was not attractive. Then, too, Mahala needed both her parents. When Ivan proposed that he should look for a flat, she agreed. They considered two possible flats. One offered by a friend of Ivan's was just what he wanted at a price he could afford to pay. Elsie, however, said she would feel happier in the alternative flat which was in a less expensive part of London. They sat down and listened quietly for guidance. Ivan realised he was thinking of himself and not of Elsie and offered to take the flat she wanted. She admitted that she had been considering herself, and that if Ivan had set his heart on the other flat, she was willing to give up her objections to it. This method of making decisions was a far cry from the old arguments that used to go on all night. They let the matter rest for a while to see if they could find a flat acceptable to both. Some time later, when nothing else had turned up, they went to see Elsie's choice again. It was still vacant, and they took that as a sign and moved in.

Soon Ivan was invited to go to America with Dr Buchman. He asked Elsie what she thought about it, to which she replied, 'You'll go whatever I think.' But Ivan said, 'No, I don't think I will. Think it over and let me know.' She did so and said she felt he ought to go. He travelled in the United States for some months, preparing for an Assembly to be held in Los Angeles, California. Then he cabled to Elsie suggesting she should come out. To his joy she accepted. He was delighted to see her, but dismayed to discover she had been put in the same room as himself, for they had never shared a room since their reunion. She made no comment, so this was a step forward.

Frank Buchman understood the quality which Ivan and Elsie brought to even the simplest song. He regarded this as their unique contribution and often called upon them. Frequently Ivan sang patter songs from Gilbert and Sullivan, with a change of words that would have astounded Mr Gilbert. Thus *I've got a little list* became:

As I read the news each morning
And my day I must arrange
I've got a little list, I've got a little list
Of society offenders
Whose ideas may need to change.
That is if they insist, that they should still exist.
There's the chap who tells the kids at school
To do just as they please,
And every chance to disobey
Their parents they should seize,
All those who say that we should have
A 'new morality',
More sex and comfort, broadcasters
Debunking chastity.
And statesmen who talk high,
But who on living low persist.
They'd none of 'em be missed—

    they'd none of 'em be missed!

Chorus: *We've got 'em on the list—*
           we've got 'em on the list,
         And they'll none of 'em be missed,
         We're sure they'll not be missed.

The Menzies were guests at a barbecue at the home of a San Franciscan businessman. The large table that stood under the decorated trees in the garden groaned under the weight of food. The host asked Ivan to sing a song. 'It's a funny thing', he replied. 'I've just written one. We'll try it out.' Clearing a little spot among the masses of food, he stood on the table and sang his new song, *Someone's Got to be Different*. It begins:

Everyone will agree that the world's in a mess
And who you would blame might be easy to guess,
But I've found an answer to what puzzled me,
Here's something with which everyone will agree:
Someone has got to be different,
*   very different, mighty different.*
To blame other folks we're all prone,
But peace in the nation must start in the home.
No squabbles have we, now I can see
That it isn't my brother, the wife or her mother—
The one to begin with is me.

Ivan was likely to break into light-hearted song in the most unexpected places. During one of his tours in Australia he was taken by a young architect, Gordon Brown, to meet the Premier of South Australia, Mr (later Sir) Thomas Playford. Ivan arrived on his little motor scooter, chained it to a post outside the Premier's office, and went in. Within a few minutes he staggered Gordon (and possibly Mr Playford as well) by singing *Someone's Got to be Different*, interspersed with his usual light-footed frolic. Before long he had the Premier helping him with ideas to improve the last verse.

The Menzies were still in the United States when World War II broke out in September 1939. While in Seattle Ivan received a cable asking him to return to London and take on his old job as principal comedian with the D'Oyly Carte Opera Company. He and Elsie returned to England on a Dutch ship which took ten days to cross the Atlantic and then was held up for five days anchored off the Goodwin Sands while they listened to news of ships in their vicinity being sunk by magnetic mines. J C Williamson's in Australia were agitating for Ivan to return for another season, as they thought he was essential if there was to be another Gilbert and Sullivan tour. He hesitated to accept the offer, preferring to stand with his home country in wartime. He returned to the D'Oyly Carte Company, which had a successful Christmas and New Year season in Edinburgh and Glasgow. D'Oyly Carte then advised him to accept J C Williamson's offer because of the uncertain future of his own Company in wartime Britain, and he decided to do so. He got a passage on an Italian ship, the *Viminale*, which fortunately reached Fremantle just before Italy entered the war.

Elsie and Mahala were to follow later. They were offered passages on the *Ceramic*, which was being used to evacuate women and children from Britain, and cabled Ivan for his approval. He cabled back, 'Follow your guidance'. Elsie had a strong feeling that they should not go, and the sequel confirmed her growing trust in the reality of guidance. The *Ceramic* was not heard of again until after the war, when it was learnt that she had been sunk by a German torpedo and all the six hundred women and children aboard had been lost.

It was not possible for Elsie to join Ivan later, but now there was a bond between them that distance could not sever.

9

You have carried firm conviction to my hesitating heart
—HMS Pinafore

This third and longest tour of Australia and New Zealand was, if possible, even more successful than the first two. So much did the popularity of the Gilbert and Sullivan operas depend on Ivan that posters advertised 'Ivan Menzies in Gilbert and Sullivan Operas'. It was most unusual to display an individual actor's name first before that of the opera.

Again he received many requests to speak at lunches, Rotary Clubs, the Millions Club, Legacy, Rostrum, Apex, the English Speaking Union and all mannner of associations. Several times he was invited to Government House by Lord and Lady Wakehurst. The President of the Employers' Federation, Mr R C Wilson, arranged for him to address three hundred leaders of employers' and employees' organisations at a lunch which the *Country Life* magazine described as 'symbolic'. 'There is the awakening of a new spirit in this fair land of ours', the article went on to say, 'a spirit of co-operation in place of conflict, a spirit of service to mankind'.

It is hard to assess the influence Ivan Menzies had upon the life of Australia and New Zealand. Yet it is evident that he *did* affect the course of events, occasionally in recognisable ways, and often through the encouragement brought to men and women in public affairs. The governors of several states counted him among their personal friends. After hearing him, one governor wrote saying that he had been thinking of little else ever since. A few weeks later he wrote again to Ivan about his struggles in trying to apply the four absolute moral standards, saying, 'I have come to the conclusion that one must not expect to do everything at once. One fence at a time.'

A Federal election was to be held in September 1940. Australia was at war with Germany, though not as yet with Japan, and Ivan understood that in a time of crisis a nation needs to mobilise all its moral and spiritual resources. The spirit of the people needs re-inforcement. Political parties may differ on points of policy, but the people can unite in a common purpose. Ivan launched a campaign to get tens of thousands of electors to sign 'The People's Declaration', which gave expression to the idealism which he believed was still latent in the average man.

Ivan's correspondence at this period shows how much this project occupied his thinking. Whatever the subject of the letter he almost invariably ended with the statement that under separate cover he was sending a copy of 'The People's Declaration'.

The response was encouraging, and remarkably representative. In acknowledging the receipt of nearly one hundred signatures from the workers in a single company Ivan wrote: 'The support of these principles from firms such as yours encourages us to put all we have into bringing this spirit into every sphere of national life.' He went on to say that signatures from a cross-section of the community included the heads of the Roman Catholic, Anglican and Jewish Liberal Churches, heads of education, students and businessmen.

Two volumes of signatures were presented by Ivan Menzies to Mr Hugh Barnard, the member for Bass. Mr Barnard rose in the House during Question Time the next day to ask the Prime Minister (Mr Menzies) whether he had received the Declaration and drew attention to its purpose, which was to 'keep the standards of the nation high, by the people practising in their homes and businesses those principles of honesty and unselfishness which must form the foundation of a healthy Australian national life'. He further asked that it be laid on the table of the Library so that members might peruse it. The Prime Minister replied that he would comply with the request. (*Hansard*, 3 December 1940.)

In New Zealand the story was much the same as in Australia—playing to capacity houses and beating all previous records. Many nights, among the many who came to his dressing-room after the show there would be at least one Cabinet Minister.

A young man, Mick Lennon, was at that time on the Executive of the Carpenters' Union. He had become active in the Labour movement because he felt that God wanted him to be responsible for his country and to begin to show that responsibility in his union. Ivan wrote to Mick asking him to arrange an interview for him with the Minister of Labour (Hon Paddy Webb). Mick did so, and went along with Ivan. They had just begun to talk when another Minister opened the office door and asked Mr Webb whether he was planning to attend the War Cabinet meeting just about to begin. Mr Webb replied, 'No, I've got Ivan and his friend here. Bring some of the Cabinet here for morning tea when you've finished.'

At morning tea, with half a dozen of the Cabinet present, Ivan turned to Mick and said, 'Mick, tell them your story.' Mick did so with fiery conviction. As they left, some of the men asked Mick to call on them to talk further, and with all of them a lifelong friendship began.

The day after this interview Ivan had dinner with the Prime Minister (Mr Peter Fraser) and his wife at the Waterloo Hotel. They moved into the lounge to meet some of Ivan's friends, Mick Lennon among them. It was a merry evening. Ivan kept things rolling along, with the Prime Minister joining in the singing of some of the songs. Mr Fraser said to Ivan later, 'Give me half a dozen more men like Mick Lennon and I'll come full time MRA myself.'

Much of Ivan Menzies' activity was concerned with maintaining morale as World War II intensified. He made many visits to military camps to give talks, or sing Gilbert and Sullivan songs and others he had written himself. He took the initiative to get civic leaders to follow the example of the Mayors of Bristol and other cities in Britain who had issued a leaflet to their citizens: 'Morale: How to Play Your Part'. In Palmerston North the Mayor declared in a radio address: 'We have an opportunity in Palmerston North to give the lead to the whole of New Zealand by introducing the spirit of MRA into our civic and individual life.'

The challenge given by Ivan cut quite deep with some men. In Christchurch a grocer who had been breaking the law by trading after hours wrote to the Chief Inspector in the Department of Labour, admitting what had been happening, and putting himself entirely in the

Inspector's hands to make any restitution he deemed necessary. Soon after the Minister of Labour wrote to Ivan about it and said, 'I cannot let this opportunity pass without conveying to you not only my own appreciation but the appreciation of my fellow Ministers for the very excellent service you have rendered the cause of humanity through your broadcasts and meetings.'

On his last day in Wellington some of the Cabinet and Members of Parliament gave a tea party for the Company. The next morning, when Ivan was due to leave Wellington at eight o'clock, the Prime Minister rang him at 7.15 to thank him and the Company for bringing laughter and music into the country, and to express his gratitude for all his work for Moral Re-Armament both inside and outside the theatre.

Whether in New Zealand or back in Australia, Ivan moved at a terrific pace. From one city he wrote, 'Even on Saturday, which contained two heavy shows of *The Yeomen of the Guard*, besides a busy morning with letters and personal talks I managed to fit in a luncheon party and after the evening performance a party in my sitting-room at the hotel for the Press and their wives. We could not get them off the premises, and it was 3 am before I got to bed.'

He was once asked what drugs he took to keep going at such a pace.

'I only take spirit', he replied in that slightly enigmatical way in which he led enquirers on.

'Do you?' the man continued. 'What spirit?'

'The Holy Spirit', Ivan answered, 'and it's never let me down. There's no hang-over.'

To compensate for his late, stimulating nights, Ivan

always went to bed from 5 pm to 6.30 pm to make sure he was fit to give his best performance at the theatre. Then the evening meal was ordered, a brief shower taken, and he was off to the theatre. If the current opera allowed him a reasonable time off stage without any change of costume his secretary would go in after he was ready and made up, and work on the day's letters. Ivan made a disciplined use of every minute. His Brisbane secretary, Hilary Bates, tells how she sometimes went into the wings with him while he was still dictating a letter. At the last moment he would say, 'Meet me on the other side', go on stage and become Sir Joseph Porter or the Duke of Plaza-Toro, then come off and say, 'Where are we?' and go on dictating.

Ivan's pride and joy was a little motor scooter which he took up in the lift with him and kept in the safety of his bedroom, standing on a sheet of newspaper. The scooter gave him a chance to get out of the city into the country air. The mountains to the east of Melbourne are conveniently near for anyone who wants to escape for a quiet weekend, and Ivan enjoyed going to a small cottage at Mt Dandenong. Using his scooter he could have two days in the mountain air before returning for the Monday night performance at the theatre. Not that he was idle. There were always letters to write, radio scripts to prepare, and talks for all kinds of occasions— a Rotary luncheon, a church service, a school assembly, as well as articles for newspapers and magazines.

Friends sometimes came to help him. Tom Uren, a young business executive, had spent the day with him, and they walked down together for Tom to catch the bus to the railway station. As he sat down and stretched his long legs (he was well over six feet tall), Ivan said gravely to Mr Jeeves, the bus driver, 'Look after my little boy, please, and set him down at the station.' The girls in the back seat, the only other passengers, began to giggle. Then to Tom's further embarrassment, as the driver shifted the gear-handle to move off, Ivan leant across to him from the doorway and added, poker faced, 'And see that he doesn't stand on the seat.' Mr Jeeves nodded, the girls giggled more loudly, Tom shuffled uncomfortably in his seat. Living with a comedian is not all fun.

When Ivan moved to Sydney the scooter often took him to one of the surfing beaches. The only lunch he needed for these outings was a bunch of bananas. Being a little weary of hotel life, he took a flat on the Harbour front at Elizabeth Bay. Here the mosquitoes were particularly troublesome to his uninitiated English constitution, and bites swelled into lumps that interfered with the light-footed dancing that was so much a part of his stage performance. Not to be beaten he made door and window frames of net that made his room look like a cage, in which he slept undisturbed.

At this time a new book written by Peter Howard was published. Peter Howard was one of Lord Beaverbrook's top journalists and had collaborated in writing a book denouncing Britain's politicians of the pre-war period, entitled *Guilty Men*. Soon after its publication he went to investigate the inner workings of Moral Re-Armament. He certainly uncovered its secrets, and he became so convinced by what he discovered that he published another book, which he called *Innocent Men*. Now there really was something to recommend in answering the fan mail. Ivan's ingenuity found other ways of promoting the book. *The Sorcerer* was the opera playing at the time, with Ivan in the name part. As he descended into hell in the last act, the audience was amazed to see that he was reading a specially designed giant copy of *Innocent Men*. The Press headlined the incident and said without truth that he had been reprimanded by the management. There was a great demand for the book next day. He got his secretary to ring the press to say he would be repeating the act that night. More headlines appeared, more alleged defiance of The Firm, more sales of the book. The book continued to be a part of the act. The back stage, or in this case the below stage, crew took a hand in the game by shooting Ivan up in the air with a mighty bump, as they returned the trap-door, bearing the notice 'house full' or 'too hot to hold'.

During a run of *The Gondoliers* the chorus joined a general strike which had been started in the Australian theatres. The principals decided to continue as best they could, and the audience was told they could either stay or have their money refunded. Most of them stayed. Edna, his secretary at the time, was standing in the wings watching the gondola being prepared for the Duke and Duchess of Plaza-Toro and suite—except that there wasn't any suite. 'I'll take my secretary on', said Ivan. Edna fled.

She was not so fortunate on the day Ivan was invited to speak at a Pleasant Sunday Afternoon in the Lyceum Theatre, Sydney, which was then owned by the Central Methodist Mission. Edna relates: 'My husband and I arrived with Ivan to find the theatre packed to the doors

Sir Robert Menzies,
Prime Minister of Australia,
1939-1941, talks backstage with
Ivan Menzies after a
performance of
The Gondoliers at
His Majesty's Theatre,
Melbourne

John Curtin, Prime Minister
of Australia, 1941-1945,
arranged for the MRA revue
Battle For Australia
to be performed in the
Parliament Dining Room
in 1943

Elsie and Ivan, united again, at a reception in South Africa, May 1954
photo: © Natal Daily News

Playwright and author Peter Howard *(top right)* **and Ivan Menzies chat with friends**
photo: Arthur Strong

Mahala, daughter of Elsie and Ivan Menzies

with probably a thousand people. We were greeted by an usher and practically danced down the aisle to the strains of the organ playing *Dear Little Buttercup*. We imagined there must be reserved seats for us at the front; but no, on we went right up on the platform to sit at the right hand of the guest speaker in the very front row.

'I was quite relaxed and happily listening to Ivan talking for about twenty minutes, when I heard him say, "I have my secretary with me today. I'm sure she'd like to say a few words to you." Loud applause. There was no way of escape from an impromptu talk to a thousand people.'

The happiness of these days was now shattered by the news that the Japanese had bombed Pearl Harbour. Sydney was immediately plunged into a black-out, for fear that it might be the next target for attack.

The Japanese advanced rapidly and when Singapore fell, our hearts fell too. One controversial action of Ivan's was to refuse to play in *The Mikado* because he felt it must offend the Japanese and increase the suffering of Australian prisoners-of-war. So during the war that opera had to be played without him. He defended his decision by quoting from letters received from parents of soldiers killed in the war, who no longer regarded *The Mikado* as amusing. He also said that when the time came to make peace with Japan he wanted to be one of those to take Moral Re-Armament to that country. As it turned out, he did have a leading role in a musical production, *The Vanishing Island*, which was taken to Japan in 1955, and which had a significant effect on Japanese policy.

10

Into Parliament you shall go
—Iolanthe

The Japanese attack on Pearl Harbour in December 1941 was followed by a southwards advance at incredible speed. As 1942 progressed the threat to Australasia became increasingly grave. The sinking of the two British battleships *Repulse* and *Prince of Wales*, followed quickly by the fall of Singapore, which Australians had been brought up to believe was an impregnable fortress, shattered the illusion that Australia could continue to shelter under the protection of the British Navy. The Japanese landed in New Guinea and advanced towards Port Moresby. It was a dark hour. Then the defeat of the Japanese Navy by the American Fleet in the Battle of the Coral Sea lightened the darkness, and the presence of the US forces under General MacArthur helped to restore confidence to a people whose homeland was being threatened for the first time in its history. It is against this background of uncertainty and apprehension that Ivan Menzies' contribution to morale should be viewed.

Mrs Beryl Mayor, known professionally as Beryl Bryant, had a small theatre in Sydney where she gave instruction in dramatic art, and produced plays of high quality (Shakespeare, Ibsen, Shaw and others). As Christmas drew near in 1941 and the Australian summer began to make itself felt, Ivan and others had been swimming in Vaucluse Bay, an inlet of the harbour, and were sipping cool drinks in Beryl's garden. Some-one remarked, 'You know that in the USA they have produced a revue called *You can Defend America*, which American leaders say is strengthening national morale. Why don't we do something like that here?'

Everyone gasped at the idea, but it began to appeal. The revue would be called *Battle for Australia*. There was fear that Australia would be invaded by the Japanese. One sketch was to show that Australia was already being invaded by 'white ants' of fear, hate, greed, disunity.

The Lord Mayor of Sydney saw the revue in Beryl Bryant's playhouse, and was so enthusiastic that he offered to sponsor other showings. The Governor of New South Wales (Lord Wakehurst), the Premier and Cabinet Ministers, Members of Parliament and Church leaders came to see it. Lord Wakehurst went especially to Newcastle to arrange with the Mayor for showings. As the most important steel-making centre in Australia, Newcastle was vital to the national war effort. Pro-duction was being threatened by an industrial dispute, and the Governor hoped that *Battle for Australia* would create a spirit in which a settlement of this dispute could take place.

The effect of the revue was seen in the action of Mr Arthur Calwell (soon to become the Federal Minister for Information) who rose to speak after the final curtain. Politicians do not easily apologise, and the audience was moved when Mr Calwell said that he owed an apology to Lord Wakehurst for derogatory remarks he had made about him in Parliament that week. Later, in Melbourne, Mr Calwell invited Ivan

Menzies and some of the cast to his home, where they produced several scenes from the revue for some of his friends among the Catholic hierarchy.

It happened that a Joint Parliamentary Committee on Broadcasting was meeting in Newcastle at the time of the revue, and accepted an invitation to attend. Some stayed until nearly midnight discussing it, and asked for it to come to Canberra. Mr D Watkins, Member for Newcastle, later wrote to the Prime Minister, saying that he had found 'a great deal of value in the production' and suggesting that the Prime Minister might issue an invitation to Mr Ivan Menzies to bring his cast to Canberra so that other members of the Commonwealth Parliament might see it.

The Prime Minister had already seen the revue. One evening, Ivan relates, he and his wife came to his dressing-room. Mr Curtin came quickly to the point. He had heard about *Battle for Australia* and would like to see it. When could he? Ivan replied that a special showing would be put on for him the following Sunday. The Prime Minister was delighted with the revue and asked where it was going to be shown next. 'I'm not sure', Ivan said. 'What about Canberra?' Mr Curtin nodded: 'Yes, I think that is the place.'

So when the letter from the Member for Newcastle arrived, this was enough to spur him into action. He suggested dates and said he would have a stage built in the Members' Dining Room at Canberra House, and would arrange for both Houses to adjourn especially for the occasion. He invited Ivan and Beryl Bryant to stay with him at the Prime Minister's residence, and offered to see that the rest of the cast were accommodated in homes as he had heard that the hotels were full.

Things were moving fast. The cast had to move too. Almost all were in jobs or professions or even in the Services; some in Sydney, others in Melbourne. Transport in wartime was difficult and restricted. Mr Curtin asked the Minister for Transport to issue permits for the members of the cast who would have to travel from Melbourne. Ivan's Company released him for a week; men and women in jobs were released by their employers; men in the Services obtained special leave.

The Prime Minister wrote also to the President of the Senate and the Speaker of the House of Representatives with suggestions for the showing of the revue, and sent invitations to the Governor-General (Lord Gowrie) and members of the diplomatic corps. To occasional criticism from the Opposition he replied that this was a uniting force above party, class, race, creeds or points of view; it was as essential as material armament and the critics would do better to get behind and help.

The unbelievable had happened; the stage had been built in the Dining Room, the cast had overcome difficulties of leave and transport, the Houses had adjourned, and the legislators of the Commonwealth waited for the show to begin. Ivan Menzies introduced it, and crept to the back of the audience to note the reactions. 'I marvelled at the miracle being enacted', he wrote later. 'I felt a mighty movement of the Holy Spirit.'

At the final curtain the Prime Minister rose and said he wanted the whole of Australia to see the show. Cries of 'Hear, hear!' 'Well', he said, 'in that case we have got to help make that possible and I invite Ivan Menzies and some of his friends to meet with me and members of my Cabinet in my room to discuss how best to do that.' In the discussion that followed Mr Curtin proposed that the revue be filmed. He offered all the equipment for making government documentary films, the services of the film producer (Charles Chauvel) if he was willing (as he was), and all the money needed. Letters continued to pass between the Prime Minister and Ivan, but in the end the practical difficulties of bringing the cast together from their jobs a thousand miles apart were found to be too great, and the film was never made. But, as the *Melbourne Age* reported (1 March 1943), history *had* been made by the performance in Parliament.

Knowing that Dr Malcolm Mackay, Minister for the Navy in the Commonwealth Parliament, 1970-71, had been closely associated with Ivan Menzies in his earlier days, we asked him recently what effect Ivan had had upon his life. He immediately became enthusiastic. With other young men from the university in Adelaide, Malcolm often called to see Ivan at the Richmond Hotel at about eight o'clock in the morning. There was Denys Lloyd, then a law student, and Frank Collins, well above average height and weight, with a booming bass voice to match his figure. They talked over with Ivan their plans for life-changing action in the university.

On one occasion Frank had been invited to address the students on Moral Re-Armament. The opposition—'Moral De-Armers', as they called themselves—were set on having some fun, which was to end with dumping Frank in the nearby river, despite his size and reputation as a boxer. The hall was packed, with a section of the audience hostile and very noisy. In the midst of their deliberate disturbance Frank, with the same unexpectedness as Ivan often displayed, sat down and listened for guidance. His thought was to appoint two ringleaders of the noisy element as chief 'chuckers-out' of anyone who caused trouble. The crowd was so surprised that from then on Frank was given a good hearing and no one needed to be thrown out. So far from being tossed into the river he was asked by the editor of the Union paper to write an article on *How to Begin*, and this was published on the front page.

When war came to the Pacific at the end of 1941, Denys joined the Army and Malcolm the Navy. Whenever his ship came into an Australian port where the Gilbert and Sullivan Opera Company were playing Malcolm linked up with Ivan.

One day Ivan took Malcolm with him to visit the Prime Minister. Mr Curtin was ill and lay on a green leather day-bed in his office. He talked to Ivan in a most intimate way about the tensions of his office and the struggles going on within his Party, and their effect upon himself. Malcolm felt it was Ivan's spiritual vitality that attracted a man of John Curtin's calibre and invited his confidence.

After leaving the Prime Minister, Ivan introduced Malcolm to the Hon Norman Makin, the Minister for the Navy and Munitions, probably more because Malcolm was in naval uniform than because of any inkling that he would one day be Minister for the Navy in a Liberal Government. Mr Makin was a close friend of Mr Curtin and in a position to observe his development as a leader under the exceptionally heavy stress of his office as wartime Prime Minister. When we talked to him recently, he told us he had watched John Curtin gain a quality of saintliness that gave him an intuition no other man had at that time. He said that one of the men who contributed much to the change in Mr Curtin's inner feelings and thinking was his secretary, Mr Fred McLaughlin, a man of firm Christian faith. Others were the Rev Hector Harrison, Presbyterian minister of St Andrew's Church, Canberra, and Ivan Menzies.

The friendship that had developed between Mr Curtin and Ivan meant much to both men. As a guest in the Prime Minister's home at the time of the revue Ivan appreciated the warmth of his hospitality. Mr Curtin played billiards very well, much better than his guest. One day he remarked, 'Your billiards are not as good as your MRA', to which Ivan replied, 'I spend more time on MRA than on billiards.'

Mr Curtin felt keenly the sorrows that war brought to so many people. There were times when he came to Ivan in deep distress, with letters from broken-hearted mothers of soldiers who had died while in Japanese hands. 'What do I do about this?' he would ask in anguish. Ivan replied that he would hesitate to tell him what to do, because he lacked the fuller knowledge that he possessed. But in his own experience he had proved that when he needed strength and direction he found them in listening to the Inner Voice. He was confident that God would speak to a Prime Minister as clearly as to an actor.

In a speech broadcast to the nation at a critical time in the war, Mr Curtin said:

'The strength of a nation is determined by its people, and so in this hour of peril, I call on everyone to examine themselves honestly, and having done so, to go to their tasks guided by a new conscience, and a new realisation of their responsibilities to their nation, and to each member of it. By so doing, we shall be a nation which is morally and spiritually re-armed, and be adequate to meet not only the tasks of war, but also the tasks of peace.'

A young RAAF trainee, Allan Griffith, also met Ivan at this time. The shy rookie, in his ill-fitting uniform, appeared at Ivan's door one night. He was convinced by Ivan's refreshing honesty and as a result made fundamental decisions that have affected his life ever since. After the war Allan entered the Public Service. For some years he has been First Assistant Secretary in the Prime Minister's Department, and has served a number of Prime Ministers.

Allan's decision to join Ivan in his battle was clinched by the gathering in the Melbourne Town Hall on the National Day of Prayer. A huge crowd of three to four thousand had packed into the hall and every seat right to the back of the gallery was filled. Ivan Menzies was the guest speaker. He gave a stirring address that many still remember. Allan was one of those who were never the same afterwards.

The revue *Battle for Australia*, which originated in Sydney, had its counterpart in Melbourne. Its success there depended very much upon the hard work put into it by Ivan Menzies to raise the standard of an obviously amateur production. He attended many of the rehearsals, infusing them with his enthusiasm and applying his professional skill, always with infectious humour. On one occasion an air-raid shelter scene was not moving quickly enough to satisfy him. Bombs were falling, the night was filled with noise and terrified voices shouted through the darkness, yet the tempo was too slow to be effective.

'Get a move on, get a move on!' Ivan urged. 'If this was a real show you'd turn the lights on and find the audience had left.'

On the nights when the revue was being presented in the functions room at Menzies Hotel, on the corner of William and Bourke Streets, the point at which Ivan was to appear and take his part was carefully worked out to fit in with the time when he was off the stage for a whole act in the opera *Princess Ida* in which he then happened to be playing at His Majesty's Theatre in Exhibition Street. He would leave the stage, slip into a suit, sometimes without removing his stage costume, dash off to Menzies Hotel, and walk on to the stage there as calmly as though he had been waiting in the wings all the evening.

One night he began by telling the audience he was not feeling well. 'I've got a bad leg', he confided mournfully, and gently pulled up the leg of his trousers, revealing the bandages which were a part of his make-up for *Princess Ida*.

His friends in the revue felt the strain of getting him back to his theatre in time for his re-entry. It was hair-raising, but somehow he always managed it.

The whole Gilbert and Sullivan Opera Company

served the war effort in many ways. They gave generously of their talents at war-loan rallies and functions to raise money. Ivan himself received a citation for special services to the Comforts Fund. Their cheerful operas seen by thousands of Australian, New Zealand and American troops on leave made a valuable contribution. A flag-draped box was always available at the theatre for General Douglas MacArthur and his staff, and his wife and son were often seen there. At one performance of *The Pirates of Penzance*, when tension over the set-backs in the war was very strong, Ivan Menzies added a verse to the Major-General's song, extolling General MacArthur, and this was received with loud applause. 'And nobody', he says, 'accused me the next day of departing from tradition.'

When Ivan left Melbourne in 1945 he was given a farewell luncheon. The United Nations Organisation was then in the process of formation, and one of the speakers at the luncheon, Mr C Morgan, MHR, paid Ivan this tribute: 'At UNCIO the delegates are building a machine. But it's one thing to build a machine and another to make it work. It needs the kind of spiritual oil and moral fuel that Ivan Menzies puts to us to make it work.'

Ten years had passed since Ivan had come to Australia. This decade was a formative period. The nation had struggled out of the Depression of the thirties to move into the war of the forties. In the effort to preserve its independence it began to find its identity more clearly. What Ivan Menzies brought strengthened the national leaders and also helped to sustain the spirit of the people.

Perhaps the best evaluation of his contribution was given in the magazine *Country Life:*

The departure of Mr Ivan Menzies marks ten years of a unique and fruitful association between an outstanding personality and a whole nation. Ivan Menzies has won a place all his own in the hearts and lives of a very large number of Australians, both through his portrayal of the immortal Gilbert and Sullivan roles and even more through his sustained and sacrificial effort to bring home to the people of Australia a sense of their true destiny.

11

Come what may, it must endure
— The Sorcerer

Meeting Ivan Menzies could be entertaining or it could be embarrassing—and there was no predicting which it would be. Jim Coulter, a young Western Australian, found it embarrassing. With a number of friends he met Ivan in his suite at the Adelphi Hotel in Perth one night after the show. 'What do you do?' Ivan asked him. Jim told him he was a cadet reporter on the *Western Australian*, Perth's morning paper, and was startled by Ivan's next question, 'How many meet with you each morning to find God's destiny for that paper?' He faltered and murmured that he took time to read the Bible each morning with his half-sister.

'Fine, fine', said Ivan, 'but what I'd like to know is who is working with you to find God's plan for that paper?'

Jim realized that Ivan had scored a direct hit.

Some years later when he went to Europe he was met by Ivan, who insisted on carrying his bags and looked after his every need. They shared a room. It was late as they prepared to retire on the first night.

'Do you want to say your prayers?' Ivan asked.

'Yes', said Jim.

'Well, let's not be too long about it', Ivan pleaded. 'You take the southern hemisphere and I'll take the northern.'

It is not recorded which one finished first.

Ivan's methods of bringing people to face the need for change were at least never dull or stereotyped. It was the unexpectedness of what he said or did that sometimes jolted the hearer into action. At the Menzies Hotel in Melbourne he often had long talks with Fred, the bureau clerk, late at night when he returned from the show, and did his best to meet Fred's ingenious arguments. After many nights, when he seemed to be making no headway, Ivan said, 'I'm fed up, and I'm not going to stay out of my bed any longer for you to argue against what you should know by now is the truth. But just so that when you die and may be tempted to tell them at the locked gates that no one told you the truth, and get me into trouble too, will you please sign this piece of paper?'

He produced a sheet of notepaper on which he had written, 'This is to certify that when I die and reach the gates of heaven, I won't say that no one told me the truth, if the gates are locked and they won't let me in, and especially I will not say that Ivan Menzies never told me.' Fred looked rather shocked but took a pen and signed the paper. Ivan went off to bed with the remark, 'Now I've got evidence, so you can't blame me.'

For several nights he went straight to the lift without stopping to talk to the clerk, until one night Fred hurried out of his office and said, 'Will you please give me back that chit I signed?'

'Oh, no, you're not going to catch me like that', Ivan replied. 'I thought it was just a joke', Fred pleaded.

'It's no joke for me', the unyielding Ivan said, and went off to bed.

The sequel of the story must wait until either Fred has been allowed to pass through the pearly gates, or Ivan arrives there with his indemnifying document.

His methods might be unusual, but his message was unmistakable. It was no light thing he asked men and women to do, and it is not surprising that some hesitated as they counted the cost.

As Robert Browning's Bishop Blougram says:

> No, when the fight begins within himself
> A man's worth something. God stoops o'er his head,
> Satan looks up between his feet—both tug—
> He's left, himself, in the middle; the soul wakes
> And grows.

A young journalist got into conversation with him in the billiard room. Round and round the table they paced as the young man struggled to make up his mind on the issues involved. Finally God won the tug-of-war and the two men knelt on the floor and prayed.

If Ivan Menzies' effect upon people was only the impact of a dynamic personality, it would have lasted only as long as he was there. But this is not so. Forty years have passed since he came to Australia and in all the states there are men and women who accepted his challenge and are still active today.

Take Bill Coffey. He was a young architect just out of Melbourne University, when he read *For Sinners Only* and wrote to Ivan. He had no thought of seeing the star of the theatre, but to his surprise Ivan phoned and suggested it.

The only time they could fit in was seven o'clock in the morning. When Bill arrived at the hotel, in considerable trepidation, Ivan was waiting fully dressed, having had his hour of quiet, although it must have been one o'clock before he had got to bed. Bill recalls two things Ivan did. He told him what kind of life he had lived before his change, and he asked him whether he had ever read the Sermon on the Mount. Bill replied evasively that he knew of it.

'Well', said Ivan, 'You read it overnight, and if you think you want to live that way, come and see me again tomorrow morning.'

That evening Bill read the Sermon on the Mount, and found it fascinating. The next morning Ivan asked, 'Would you like to give your life to God?' Bill did so.

Ivan believed that when a man started a new life he needed to declare it immediately. He sent Bill off to work with assorted literature in his hand. His colleagues at the office, a fairly bohemian group Bill calls them, wanted to know what he was carrying, and he was forced to tell them of the decision he had just made. As he expected, they greeted this with loud guffaws. But Bill kept to his convictions.

Then there is Jeff Warren. He met Ivan in Sydney late in 1935. His sixteen-year-old sister had appeared in a film and the family was giving a party in Romano's night club to celebrate her success. Ivan was invited. Despite a heavy day at the theatre with a matinee and an evening performance, he put on his double-breasted dinner suit—a style then in advance of Australian fashion—and went off to the party. Jeff does not remember a word that was said, but he became aware of Ivan's tranquillity and his warmth of interest in him as a person.

A scene from *The Vanishing Island*, in which
Ivan Menzies played King Capricorn

Left to right: Ole Olsen, Ivan Menzies, Surya Sena,
and Reginald Owen, who took part in *The Vanishing Island*
at Geneva in 1955 during the World Mission

Ivan and Elsie Menzies on their Golden Wedding Day,
with gifts which they gave to the Westminster Theatre

As Ivan departed he invited Jeff, his two sisters and and another young man to *The Yeomen of the Guard*. They enjoyed it immensely. Ivan gave them the impression that he was enjoying some huge joke and was trying to get it across to the audience as he bounced around the stage with the resilience of a golf ball. At supper afterwards he was equally resilient. Future meetings led Jeff to the same decision as Bill Coffey had made.

Jeff worked with a secondhand car dealer. When he stood by what he thought to be absolute honesty, he was sacked. This seemed a calamitous start, but to his amazement, Ivan hooted with delight at the news. Obviously God wanted him out of that job, and at the right time would show him what He wanted him to do. Meanwhile he could share his flat, and work as his secretary. Jeff remained with him during the rest of the Australian tour, and then accompanied him to New Zealand.

In Adelaide in 1936 someone suggested to a young architect, Gordon Brown, that he should meet Ivan Menzies. He remembers that meeting well:

'It was a Sunday morning, with a hot north wind blowing. I called for him in my motor car—an old open Morris—and drove down to the seaside, where we began to walk up and down the beach. We were complete strangers, but Ivan began to tell me many things that were deep in his life. I was at that time superintendent of one of the biggest Sunday Schools in the state. But for a man to be as frank as Ivan was took me somewhat by surprise. The other thing that shook me was that the things he talked about applied to me also. There was something about him, his gaiety, sincerity and obvious care for me as a person that I had never quite come across before.

'We drove to the city around midday. I pulled my car up in front of the Botanic Hotel on North Terrance, one of Adelaide's main thoroughfares. There were streams of people walking past to the Botanic Gardens. Ivan suddenly said, 'Now you have told me some of the things on which you need victory. We can't do this without God's help. Would you like to pray with me?'

' "What!" I exclaimed. "Here in the street with everybody passing?" He said calmly, "Why not?", and immediately put his head down and started to pray. I cocked an eye to see if anybody was watching, and then joined in. It was there that I first committed myself to God without reserve.'

Gordon built up a successful business as an architect, on the principle that human relationships came first and profits were not to be amassed for himself but be spent as God directed for the remaking of the world. In 1965 he became interested in Rajmohan Gandhi's vision for an MRA training centre at Panchgani in India. He offered his services as an architect, visiting Panchgani nine times in ten years to supervise the work as the buildings were planned and erected stage by stage. All the architectural drawings, worth many thousands of dollars at normal rates, were donated by the firm of Brown, Davies, Reynolds & Dole.

If the tens of thousands who come to Panchgani knew the full story of how it came into being, they might sometimes see in the wings of its beautiful theatre a shadowy figure of an actor who forty years earlier brought inspiration to a young architect in Australia.

When John Williams first met Ivan at a lunch he was still at school. He has always remembered Ivan's saying that everything in a day was likely to go wrong if he missed listening to God first thing in the morning.

Some months later John was taking part in his school production of *Iolanthe*. On the opening night he had a telegram from Ivan: 'Good luck from one Lord Chancellor to another'. John relates, 'When I heard a month or two later that Ivan was returning to Sydney, I decided to give the experiment of listening to God a try. Many relationships and facts about life on which I was confused fell into place. When I saw him, he didn't try to convert or persuade me. He just told me his experience and I was convinced by his infectious joy. During the next four years I received every few months an almost illegible postcard or letter from Ivan in the different capitals he was visiting.'

These stories of individuals are only a few of the many that could be told. Australians are to be found today in many parts of the world working for a just society that reflects God's plan for mankind. Some of these are men and women who were directly inspired and changed by Ivan Menzies many years ago; others are their sons and daughters.

12

Let's look for something new
—The Vanishing Island

In his early twenties Ivan consulted a fortune-teller at a country fair. She gazed into her crystal ball and said, 'I see you becoming a great success in the theatre'. Ivan's pulse quickened, for that was his dearest wish.

'I see you sailing a long way in a big ship and being a great success', she continued. This was more exciting still.

'Then', she concluded, 'I see you connected with a new kind of theatre and teaching people a new art.'

By 1945, when Ivan left Australia for America, the first two parts had come true and, amazingly, the rest of his life was to be concerned with fulfilling the third part.

In his professional career he had seen the power of drama to move people to laughter and tears. Might it do more? In seeing the follies and weaknesses of men and women on the stage, might they realise their own? Often an audience would be stirred to a desire for a better life after seeing a play where right triumphed over wrong. How could this feeling be made to last beyond a few hours after a show and be translated into action?

Ivan believed strongly in what a group working together could do. *Battle for Australia* had affected the life of that country at a critical time. Now in the post-war world there were urgent needs in many nations.

He now met an international group who were already at work experimenting with a new type of theatre. They had begun production in an old wooden barn on the island of Mackinac, where the lakes Michigan and Huron meet. Their first show had been the wartime revue *You Can Defend America* which had given the idea for *Battle for Australia*. Ivan was delighted to work with them. One musical operetta *The Statesman's Dream* seemed to him a logical sequence to the Gilbert and Sullivan operas.

Ivan was in his element. His activities took many forms. He enjoyed coaching the teenagers who put on shows for schools and colleges. It was sometimes tough-going. On one occasion, just before the curtain was due to rise the two principal players got into a violent fight. Ivan grabbed them, banged their heads together and made them have a 'compulsory' time of quiet! The curtain went up and they gave a brilliant show.

One industrial drama, *The Forgotten Factor* by Alan Thornhill, produced at this time is still playing to great effect in many parts of the world. In London it was produced at the Westminster Theatre. This theatre had been purchased as a memorial to men and women who had given their lives in the war and was dedicated on Remembrance Sunday 1946 to present 'the plays of the new renaissance to fashion the world they died to bring'. Ivan was among the first to see the possibilities of a theatre whose aim was 'to provide a constructive drama of ideas relevant to the post-war world and based on Christian faith and morals'. He involved himself fully in the development of these plays and has done so ever since.

He made a final tour of Australia with the Gilbert and Sullivan operas. This was in 1950-51. During the previous tour Elsie had been looking after her parents who were ill but this time she went with him. She was thrilled at the tumultuous welcome he received. In several of the cities they rented a small house or flat where Elsie was able to help Ivan to entertain their friends.

While he was playing in Melbourne, an Australian cast was rehearsing in *The Forgotten Factor* for a New Zealand tour. Elsie trained the chorus of girls who sang before the play opened. During the war Australia and New Zealand had been moving towards a realisation of their nationhood. How could this patriotic feeling be retained? Both countries had a wealth of natural resources of which they could justly be proud. With this in mind Elsie designed special costumes for the chorus in a variety of plain colours, with unusual embroidery on the skirts. Each featured a design that would express the cultures of the two countries—yellow wattle, pink flowering gum, red and black Sturt pea, the strange kangaroo paw, the boomerang and animals such as the koala bear. No wonder the audience gasped and burst into applause when the curtain went up.

In 1952 Dr Buchman invited Elsie and Ivan Menzies to join a team of over 200 people whom he was taking to India on an invitation from a national committee of Indian leaders. They acted in plays and sang in many parts of India during the six months' tour. In Delhi, Prime Minister Nehru, who had enjoyed Gilbert and Sullivan operas when at Oxford, was delighted to meet Ivan, who sang him many songs from the operas.

To this day there are many from all over India who have never forgotten that visit—people for whom it meant new life, new relationships in industry, new unity in the family, new attitudes to servants and new love of country.

Among the team was Peter Howard, the British author whose book *Innocent Men* Ivan had displayed from the stage during performances of *The Sorcerer*. Peter Howard's daughter wrote of the lasting effect this journey had on her father's life and writing. 'It made him increasingly aware of the need to answer the vast problems of continents. This expansion of his thinking led to his beginning to write plays for the theatre, something he had never before attempted.' * Often he wrote his plays with Ivan in mind, and would talk them over with him and others of his friends.

Ivan and Elsie both had key parts in *The Real News*, Peter Howard's first play. In *Pickle Hill* Ivan played the part of Bill Pickle, the college bootlegger, and wrote the opening song with which Bill makes his entry. Peter Howard called him a born lyricist and urged him to write an operetta in Gilbert and Sullivan style. He and Ivan had a life-long friendship. Both had the same directness of approach, fearlessness of challenge and impish sense of humour.

Ivan had sold his Pacific Island, Bedarra, for £500, the sum he gave for it. Besides the visions of pleasure it evoked, Bedarra had also been the symbol of his despair that normal life could ever really be satisfying. He had now done with 'dream islands', as reality was all-absorbing and fascinating.

*Wolrige Gordon, Anne: *Peter Howard, Life and Letters* Hodder and Stoughton 1969

But another island was to appear on his horizon. Peter Howard wrote a musical play, *The Vanishing Island*, something in the style of Gilbert and Sullivan. He had Ivan in mind for the part of King Capricorn, the constitutional monarch of the island of Eiluph'mei (I love me) where liberty had turned to licence. Its people are hated by those of Weiheit'ui (we hate you), a country with a totalitarian dictatorship. A delegation sent by King Capricorn's cabinet to Wei'heit'tui to try to make peace fails through its arrogant approach. In their fury, the people of Weiheit'ui, led by their ambassador Odioso, put a curse on the island and it begins to disappear. Panic sets in and King Capricorn reminds his ministers of something they have forgotten. He sings:

> *There's one voice yet that the world can hear—*
> *It's the voice of courage, it's the voice of cheer—*
> *It's a voice in each heart, and it's ever near.*
> *It's the voice of the King of Kings.*

His people see the failure of their way of life, and begin to understand that the secret of peace is 'people deciding to be different'. Odioso returns. His attention is gripped as King Capricorn sings of a new hope:

> *Let's look for something new*
> *Together we from East and West can dare*
> *To rebuild the world for all men everywhere.*

The island slowly reappears and Odioso realises that the curse is broken and that hate

> *Carries within itself a certain fate*
> *To destroy the men that use it.*

The play was to be produced in Los Angeles and rehearsals began as soon as Ivan arrived. To his surprise he found that no matter how hard he tried, he couldn't get his part right. He knew something was missing. He broke down and said, 'I've been thinking I could do this because of all my experience and talent, but it is too big for me. I need the power of God to break through my egotism.' As he admitted this, something extraordinary happened. The whole play came alive and sparkling. A Hollywood producer watching him said, 'I've never seen a rehearsal like that in my life before.' Reginald Owen, a British star of Hollywood and Broadway, who was playing another leading role, said, 'If the show does that to us, what will it do to the audience?'

Looking back, Ivan says he realised at that point that it all depended on whether he wanted people to say he was wonderful or whether he was willing to empty himself and be filled with the spirit of Christ. As one of the cast said of him, he came to love the Giver more than the gift.

The Vanishing Island became an integral part of a world mission of statesmen and ordinary people, some two hundred of them, drawn from many races, who travelled right round the world. From America the mission flew to Japan, a fulfilment of what had been in Ivan's mind at the time of *The Mikado* controversy during the war. The party that moved on to the Philippines was joined by a group of Japanese politicians including Mr Hoshijima, adviser to the Japanese Cabinet. At the end of *The Vanishing Island* in Manila, Mr Hoshijima rose to speak. The hostility of the audience, many of whom had suffered at the hands of the Japanese during the war, was intense. Mr Hoshijima said: 'We must humbly apologise for the past. That is why my Prime Minister urged me to come on this Mission. Please forgive us.' The mood changed. There was a gale of applause and many Filipinos pressed forward to shake his hand. Later the Japanese Prime Minister, Mr Kishi, visited Australia and also apologised for the suffering his nation had caused.

The mission moved on to Taiwan, Bangkok, Rangoon and Calcutta, New Delhi, Colombo. Wherever it went, hearts were opened and hope began to rise. They flew on to Baghdad, Tehran, Cairo and Nairobi. The experience was rewarding, but not without discomfort. The weather was often hot and humid, King Capricorn's robes were heavy, air conditioning was rare, and planes were often delayed. Yet the pampered, temperamental actor of former days, who must always have a fan in his dressing room or he would threaten to walk out, was quite undemanding. An Australian on the mission said, 'There he was, night after night, steady and consistent, absolutely dependable.'

Passing through Turkey and the principal cities of Switzerland, the mission reached Scandinavia in December. There were three feet of snow outside the theatre. Ivan's thought was, 'Your spine won't get chilly if your heart is on fire.' But he was glad to accept one of the sheepskin coats which the Swedish army lent their visitors.

In Finland, Ivan and Elsie were received by the President and his wife. They sang to him and told how their marriage had been remade. The President and his wife got up from their gold chairs, took their hands and thanked them with tears in their eyes. There was just time before Christmas to go up to Kiruna and play in the most northerly theatre in the world.

After visits to Milan and Paris, they drove through World War I battlefields on their way to Germany. Memories crowded in on Ivan as he stood among the thousands of crosses and found the names of some of his old comrades. Now he was going into Germany with a message of reconciliation, and he wrote to a friend, 'Fancy God trusting a chap like me with a part like this.'

While in Hanover they went after the performance every night for a week to Philips' studios to record *The Vanishing Island*. Recording began at midnight and Ivan's solos, in which the clarity of enunciation is outstanding, usually came on about four o'clock in the morning.

On to Britain and across to America, where the long and unique odyssey ended. Reginald Owen wrote: 'There has been nothing like *The Vanishing Island* in theatrical history. Never has a play had such an effect on the thinking of Cabinets around the world.'

13

Ably have you played your part
—HMS Pinafore

The year 1962 was a difficult one. Elsie had a throat operation which ended her singing career. Her beautiful voice could be heard only on records. Ivan suffered a heart attack which forced him to take life more quietly. So they had to settle down in their modest home in Barnes, a suburb of London. The spotlight was no longer on them. After a lifetime as celebrities, applauded by admiring crowds, with all the excitement that fame brings, this restricted life has not been easy. In 1970, Elsie fell and broke her hip. Although a pin was inserted and she can walk again, arthritis had developed and she is in almost constant pain.

Despite their difficulties, the Menzies' home is a merry one. Mahala, who came home to care for her parents, is a chip off the old block and quite able to match her father's wit. There are arguments, as in the early days, and for a while one or other holds out for the last word. Sooner or later they will remember to sit and listen for what God has to say. Apologies follow and points of view change. Often this leads to spontaneous prayers for forgiveness or the seeking of guidance over particular problems.

Many guests pass through their home. Australians and New Zealanders are given a special welcome. Elsie is the warm-hearted hostess with something of a prima donna in the gracious way she receives her guests and

cares for every detail of their comfort. Ivan is the enter-
tainer, delighting to meet people, who become his
audience again.

Naturally, at times they think of the past. Dozens
of photos on the walls and shelves remind them of their
Gilbert and Sullivan triumphs and of celebrities they
knew. It takes new guests some time to mount the
stairs. They must look at Elsie singing in the presence
of King George and Queen Mary; they must see Ivan in
his dressing room as the Duke of Plaza Toro, talking
to Sir Robert Menzies; there are autographed photos of
John Curtin, Kingsford Smith and Rupert D'Oyly
Carte; posters that hung outside the theatres in their
hey-days; and photos of Frank Buchman and Peter
Howard, who meant so much in their lives.

But Ivan does not live on memories. He constantly
thinks and plans for the moral re-armament of the
world. He prays regularly for an amazing number of
people in all continents.

Without doubt his heart is still in the theatre, which
he sees as in the forefront of a rebirth of faith. He longs
that actors should become prophets who declare God's
truth to the world. When he and Elsie celebrated their
Golden Wedding in 1973, despite their limited means,
they did not accept gifts for themselves but asked their
friends to look through their possessions for any articles
of gold which could be used to support the Westminster
Theatre. Gifts came from many parts of the world. In
true Menzies style Ivan told his dentist about the
scheme, and was rewarded by a collection of gold
fillings removed from patients' discarded teeth. In all,
more than £2,500 was raised.

Although now eighty, Ivan will not agree that his feet have become any less nimble. 'There's nothing wrong with my feet; it's only my heart that's the trouble', he declares, as he dances round the room with hands clasped over his heart in dramatic gesture. For him there is no such thing as retirement.

'God called me to remake men and nations', he says, 'and that task is never finished.'